Testimonials

Positioning 4 Retirement is an excellent analysis of the pros and cons of having a retirement plan. Mark Cardoza has written the only treatise I know of that discusses the hazards and potential pitfalls of having a qualified retirement plan. This book should be read by everyone who has an IRA, 401(k), Contributory or Defined Benefit Pension Plan, or a Roth IRA. Well worth the reading.

Rick Solano, CPA, MST
Former Supervisory IRS Agent
Author, *The Power of a Millionaire Mentality*

In *Positioning 4 Retirement*, Mark Cardoza has shown an outstanding ability to demonstrate clearly to the reader the need for retirement planning and the many choices available when undertaking such an activity. Mark writes insightfully about the need for preparing for retirement while focusing on the potential pitfalls involved and related choices and modifications that may be required with respect to maximizing the value of income and assets and minimizing taxes. The author explains the necessity for the selection of an independent team of experts when the time comes for retirement planning and convincingly indicates it cannot come too soon in one's lifetime. He properly emphasizes that each person does indeed have individualized objectives and needs when undertaking such planning. He explains the concept of qualified funds and non-qualified funds with clarity at the beginning of the book and expands upon their meaning, use, and interacting properties throughout the text.

The author classifies financial products into proper categories throughout the text and defines and discusses annuities with clarity. The time-value of money concepts are included in the illustrations. The worksheets and spreadsheet add a wonderful dimension to the text and contribute to a clearer understanding of difficult concepts.

It is with great pleasure that I most highly recommend this outstanding text.

Mary J. Phelan, CPA, MBA, MA
Former IRS Revenue Agent
Accounting Professor, Quincy College
Research Associate, Framingham State University

Positioning 4 Retirement is an excellent guide for navigating the various issues encountered when preparing for retirement. Mark Cardoza masterfully presents important pre- and post-retirement information, case studies, and pertinent examples in an easy-to-read manner. Review questions at the end of each chapter provide the reader with a powerful tool to check understanding of the material. I have read many books related to investing and retirement. This book is by far the easiest and most comprehensive I have read.

Richard P. Payant, DBA
George Mason University

In my fifteen years as an advisor consultant, I haven't seen a more comprehensive retirement planning book than *Positioning 4 Retirement*. What makes this book so unique is how Mark Cardoza breaks every aspect of retirement planning down and explains it so that anyone can understand. This is a must-have book for pre-retirees, retirees, financial planners, along with attorneys and CPAs.

Karl Hoover
Financial Independence Group

Mark has hit a home run with *Positioning 4 Retirement*. He provides a wealth of information that will help guide anyone with his or her individualized retirement plan. After completing the worksheets and spreadsheet, you'll know exactly how well you're positioned for your own retirement.

R. Tetrault
Westport, MA

As a person quickly approaching retirement, I thought my savings and investment portfolio was right on track. After reading *Positioning 4 Retirement*, I realized my understanding was quite inadequate. The concepts of planning strategies, impact of taxes, and the vulnerability of my funds were an eye opener. Wish I'd had this valuable information twenty years ago.

Morris P.
Florida

Very informative and clearly written. Easy to focus on those areas that apply to your situation with ample references for deeper research. Nicely provides the key perspectives of investing, tax management, long-term health care, and estate planning and the need for a full team of resources to cover all of the bases. Qualified versus non-qualified plans and their impact on retirement tax management are particularly well presented. Good examples are given based on personal experience.

I would definitely recommend this book, especially for those who can get a head start on their retirement planning, e.g., people in their early forties.

Paul M.
New York

Mark Cardoza has done a wonderful job of explaining the often difficult to understand subject of money management. His style is both interesting and informative, and I especially like the way he aligns his website with the book.

J. Tetrault
Westport, MA

Funny how we all think we have this topic understood and covered ... well, until you read this book. People who are currently preparing for their future and retirement or who have already been investing need to read *Positioning 4 Retirement*. Mark has an acute awareness and knowledge of the need to understand fully all that is needed in a successful retirement. This truly was educational for me, and I couldn't put the book down. Makes you wonder what else we are missing.

I was impressed by the breadth and depth of the information and picked up a few nuggets that I wasn't aware of before. Mark's explanations are easy to consume, and I can see myself educating others. I will come back to this as reference.

Positioning 4 Retirement is an indispensable write-up of personal investments, retirement, tax lien investing, and more. Mark makes a complex subject clear and simple. The book is a pleasure to read and shows you how to approach investing in ways I have just not seen covered before. This is required reading for anyone interested in retirement and financial help.

Rick Harper
Boston, MA

POSITIONING 4 RETIREMENT

Taking Control and Planning Wisely
for Your Future

By Mark S. Cardoza

Illustrated by George A. Heath

Book Publishers Network
P.O. Box 2256
Bothell • WA • 98041
Ph • 425-483-3040
www.bookpublishersnetwork.com

10 9 8 7 6 5 4 3 2 1

Printed in the United States of America

LCCN	2015930375
ISBN	978-1-940598-56-7 (Print edition)
ISBN	978-1-940598-66-6 (eBook edition)

Legal Editor: *Lawrence S. Zaharoff, Esq.*
Tax Editors: *Gary J. Marini, CPA*
           Jack D. Adelson, CPA
           Glenn P. Cunniff, CPA
Securities Editor: *Vincent Serratore*
Editors: *Julie Scandora*
           Lisa M. Wynn
           Sharon E. Zaharoff
Cover Designer: *Laura Zugzda*
Book Designer: *Melissa Vail Coffman*
Illustrator: *George A. Heath*

To my father, Tony, and his brother, Joe.

Contents

Acknowledgements

S pecial thanks to:

My wife and soul mate, Janice, for her patience, love, and understanding; for believing in me and my achievements; and for having the will to help others with me.

My mother, Rita, and my children, Mike, Chris, and Julie, for their love, support, and encouragement.

My father, Tony, and his brother, Joe. Without their passing, I would not have entered this field and experienced many of the elements that are shared in this book, enlightening many people and more to come.

Attorney Lawrence S. Zaharoff of Zaharoff & Zaharoff for conveying his knowledge and experience. Larry's soft-spoken, gentle personality, coupled with his passion for the law and his clients, made understanding the legal world of estate and Medicaid planning much easier.

CPAs Gary J. Marini, Jack D. Adelson, and Glenn P. Cunniff of PECK Associates for taking the time to comment and focus on the tax issues, while recognizing and clarifying a complex tax world, making *Positioning 4 Retirement* easy to read and understand.

Vincent Serratore of Heritage Wealth Management for his encouragement, support, edification, and contribution. His ability to be open-minded when blending his knowledge and experience, while understanding the separation of securities and insurance, is well respected.

Graphic artist/illustrator George A. Heath for his time and attention to the detail in each drawing, illustration, and graph, and translating the content of the book through his eyes and mind to his hands into art with ease.

Lisa M. Wynn, paralegal, for her editing skills, arranging and organizing the articles in a sequence that made sense, recognizing areas that required clarification, and noting elements on the overall subject that needed to be addressed.

Sharon E. Zaharoff for her time, patience, and editing skills and for changing single, complex sentences into several more understandable and smoother-flowing ones. *Positioning 4 Retirement* would not be so easy to read and comprehend without you.

Julie Scandora for analyzing, cross-referencing, and clarifying the information presented while demonstrating the art of editing.

Dan Raymo of Platypus Multimedia Solution for designing a website to complement the book and fit our current and future needs.

Gary Fradin for sharing his writing experience, ultimately recommending the book's content to become simplified and illustrated.

Charles (Chip) Landquist for offering his patience, knowledge, experience, and mentoring skills at the very beginning of my career in the finance world.

Simon, a friend whose words, "you see things differently than others, and you should share what you see," inspired me to write this book.

Rick Solano, Karl Hoover, Mary J. Phelan, Jay and Debbie S., Richard P. Payant, Paul M., Morris P., Rick Harper, and R. and J. Tetrault for your comments and testimonials.

Sheryn Hara and her team at Book Publishers Network for taking the manuscript into the final stages and making it a reality.

Dunkin' Donuts, 1280 Belmont Street, Brockton, Massachusetts, for allowing us to use their conference space.

And to family, friends, and clients who encouraged and believed in me and what I do. Thank you for allowing me to influence your lives and use your stories.

Thank you all.

Preface

I was inspired to write *Positioning 4 Retirement* to help people make the best of their retirement, whether already at that stage or planning for it. My goal is to help them understand the intricate plans and programs for retirement and to illustrate the importance of positioning these plans to optimize control. In my experience, many people are unaware or do not understand their retirement plan, its function, the components, and how each component responds and reacts with the other parts. It is my objective to help our society better understand the programs they are working with while directing them to build a healthy retirement portfolio with options and choices to fit their goals.

Retirement planning is the process of accumulating assets that can be sold or transferred entirely or in part to create:

- income supporting everyday expenses and complementing Social Security and pensions;
- reserves for emergencies, vacations, gifts, family support, and good living while in retirement;
- protection to provide for you, your spouse, or your partner in the event of death or the need for extended care;
- an inheritance for your children.

Assets include real estate, physical property of value (such as a piece of art, a race horse, or investments) and liquid assets (such as stocks and bonds, savings, cash-value life insurance, cash on hand, CDs, etc.).

Today's society is more afraid of running out of money during retirement than dying. Leaving wealth for one's children is less of a concern than becoming a financial burden to them. This book is designed to help alleviate these concerns and to secure a lifelong retirement with the opportunity to leave assets to one's heirs.

There are four primary components to a comprehensive retirement plan:

- a financial plan for accumulation and distribution of funds
- a plan to protect income and assets from devastation and destruction
- a legal plan of individual wishes while alive and afterward
- a tax plan that coordinates the accumulation and distribution in unison with the legal plan

The four components have elements, or phases:

- The accumulation and distribution component has two common elements: investment and insurance.
- The legal plan can have several elements from a will to a sophisticated estate plan with possibly a business succession plan.
- Both the estate plan and business plan can be built and amended as the assets grow and the dynamics change.
- The tax plan is driven by the complexity of the legal plan and, thus, has elements that correspond to the legal plan.

A successful retirement plan not only should have all of these components but should also have all these parts synchronized.

Positioning 4 Retirement discusses each of these components and exposes some of the idiosyncrasies that are built into our government systems that can be detrimental to a retirement plan. But the US government also promotes programs that benefit the public, and the book includes these among the choices to help readers plan for their future.

Positioning 4 Retirement's objective is to educate so you can formulate sensible decisions that are easy to understand. The book also provides in-depth information for those looking for more comprehensive details. For this reason, following the explanatory foundation in the chapters, we have included articles that expand upon that information.

How to Get the Most Out of This Book

The chapters of the book offer simplified information meant for easy reading. The information in the chapters is from the article section, which provides a more in-depth analysis of the chapter content.

At the end of each chapter, there are questions, ensuring the reader understands the content.

At the end of each section, there are practical applications to determine how the section fits your own retirement plan, putting the section in perspective for you personally. To assist you in completing your practical applications, proceed to **www.Positioning4Retirement.com** to complete and print out the worksheets that coordinate with that section. The information continues with the website, which offers the following:

- worksheets designed to help you get organized
- a spreadsheet that brings it all together and helps you track your funds and plan your next step
- resources and contact information to access professionals you may want to talk to
- communications that will keep you informed of new ideas and information pertinent to retirement
- access to the online newsletter
- ongoing resources of retirement information

Once you have read *Positioning 4 Retirement* and followed its instructions, you should have:

- a better understanding of how to position retirement assets more effectively;
- an understanding as to government's position in regards to your retirement fund;
- an idea of the options available to balance qualified plans, offsetting government rules and regulations;
- a sense of comfort knowing you are in control of your retirement plan.

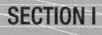

GETTING TO KNOW YOUR RETIREMENT PLAN

CHAPTER 1

Qualified Retirement Plans

The first step toward understanding your retirement plan is to identify the type of qualified plan you may have through your employer or your options for a retirement plan if you are self-employed. From my experience with organizing retirement plans, people need to have a firm understanding of qualified and non-qualified money. Understanding the difference, how they can affect your retirement, and how to manage these types of funds are critical to optimizing your retirement plan. By managing your qualified and non-qualified money properly, you can save on taxes, leaving more money to spend when and where you want.

Most people refer to their retirement plan as their 401(k), 403(b), or another tax code assigned to their plan. These retirement plans are known as **qualified** plans.

Qualified retirement plans are assigned these numbers, based on the tax code they follow. In general, these plans are driven by the employer with the help of a plan administrator. The employee has the right to participate in the plan based on the guidelines established by the organization and the US government to receive tax advantages. Oftentimes, the employer will match the employee's contribution and will receive a tax advantage as well. Each plan has elements that differentiate one from the other, such as distribution restrictions and limiting plan sponsors.

Here are the basic programs and an overview of what they offer:

- **401(k)** is for those employed by a for-profit company.
- **403(b)** is for those employed by a non-profit organization.
- **457(b)** is for employees of the government.
- **Designated Roth accounts** are unique plans offered by the employer with special tax considerations.
- **SIMPLE and SEP, including the Solo and Safe Harbor** options, are generally used with small companies and self-employed individuals. Although there are several options for self-employed individuals, total contribution is calculated on an individual basis, not by the plan. This eliminates the individual from exceeding the limits. Each plan offers tax advantages for both the employee and the employer.
  - **SIMPLE** is Savings Investment Match Plan for Employees. This type of account has tax advantages for both the employee and employer with fewer than one hundred employed. Among the advantages, the employee receives a 3 percent match while the employer is able to use the contribution as a tax deduction.
  - **SEP** stands for Simplified Employee Pension. A SEP is for self-employed individuals filing their taxes as a sole proprietor or as a partnership. Among the guidelines, the employer must contribute equally into the employee's account.
  - **Solo 401(k)**, as its name indicates, is for the self-employed individual and spouse with no full-time employees, following the same rules and requirements as a traditional 401(k).
  - **Safe Harbor 401(k)** is unique since it is not subject to annual contribution testing typical of a traditional 401(k). In exchange, employees receive a certain level of contribution based on how the plan is designed.

Generally, the functions of these qualified plans are similar, and their results are the same for employer-sponsored programs; however, the manner in which they are monitored and administered differs by the employer and plan. Each plan has its own unique quality that makes it different and adaptable to an employer. One major element that all the plans offer is tax advantages for both the employee and the employer, which makes accumulating qualified funds very attractive and inviting.

The following plans are independent from employer-sponsored plans:

- **Traditional IRA** is separate from employer plans and used independently, in addition to the above plans.
- **Roth IRA** is a unique plan that offers special tax considerations and is separate from the above plans.

One element that all the plans mentioned have in common is they are qualified plans.

Qualified Explained

The word "qualified" confuses most people when discussing retirement plans. Simply put, a qualified plan refers to an account that meets certain IRS guidelines in order to be considered a retirement account. It is also referred to as "qualified money" or a "qualified fund." Moving forward, we will refer to these plans as "qualified."

Qualified funds can be in the form of securities, such as stocks, bonds, mutual funds, CDs, and annuities. The money placed in a qualified plan has special tax considerations.

Special Tax Considerations of a Qualified Plan

The following information lists elements of qualified retirement plans.

- The money that goes into a qualified retirement fund has not been taxed and is referred to as "pre-tax dollars."
- The pre-tax dollars grow tax deferred meaning, until you take a distribution, you do not pay income taxes
- The money is taxed based on the individual's tax bracket and tax rules at the time of withdrawal. The general assumption is that the tax bracket will be lower when the individual has retired.
- Early withdrawal, before age 59½, will result in a 10 percent IRS penalty. However, there are special circumstances for withdrawals prior to age 59½ without penalty that meet IRS qualifications. These include the down payment for first-time home buyers, death of the individual, total disability, extensive medical expenses, health insurance premium while unemployed, college expenses, and others.

Consequences of Special Tax Considerations for Qualified Plans

Not paying tax on the income you earn and allowing it to grow with the funds that you would have paid in taxes causes you to be taxed on a greater portion of money. This allows the US government to be a partner in your retirement plan. Uncle Sam then has control over when and how you can spend these funds. By choosing a qualified plan, you are giving Uncle Sam the ability to mandate and establish rules, regulations, and guidelines that can change frequently and in favor of the government. Uncle Sam also has the ability to change the special tax considerations. He is in your pocket and has majority control. The only control that individuals have is how and where the funds are placed in order for them to grow. But Uncle Sam still oversees the placement of money with guidelines and regulations.

Protecting your retirement funds is not Uncle Sam's priority. Chapter 2, "The Secret behind Qualified Money," will expose the biggest and worst concerns qualified funds can present while other chapters will offer solutions to offset Uncle Sam's control.

For More Information

Please reference article 1, "What Few Know about Their 401(k) and Other Qualified Retirement Funds."

CHAPTER 1 REVIEW QUESTIONS

1. Retirement accounts are named after the IRS tax code they represent. Which of the following are proper tax codes for retirement accounts?

   A. IRA and ROTH
   B. 401(k) and 403(b)
   C. Simple and SEP
   D. All of the above

2. What is qualified money?

   A. Money that meets IRS guidelines for retirement funds.
   B. Money that is saved for retirement in a CD that is not an IRA.
   C. Money that is not yet taxed and meant for retirement.
   D. Both A and C.

3. Our money in a retirement account is mixed with government money (taxes that were deferred). Therefore, we must follow the rules, regulations, and guidelines set by the government; otherwise we will be penalized.

   TRUE   FALSE

4. The US government works hard to protect our qualified funds.

   TRUE   FALSE

CHAPTER 2

The Secret behind Qualified Money

In chapter 1, we:

- identified the titles that retirement plans are assigned;
- clarified the term "qualified" that is often used when discussing retirement plans;
- put the relationship between qualified money and the US government in perspective;
- explained that the US government makes it difficult to protect qualified money.

Now we can examine a major burden that qualified money can place on retirees if not planned properly. Chapter 2 will expose the biggest and worst concern qualified funds can present.

A commonly unknown detail, and the major point to make in this chapter, is **the vulnerability of qualified funds to be taken by the government and used for skilled long-term care needs prior to the individual accessing Medicaid.** Unless properly protected, regardless of your situation, qualified funds can and will leave your spouse and family

without the income and assets you have worked hard to build. **Failure to protect your assets can be devastating!**

Your qualified retirement funds are vulnerable for the following reasons.

- Qualified money must remain in the name and Social Security number of the person that is accumulating these funds. Doing so gives the federal government control and access to these funds for skilled nursing care (a nursing home) after the first one hundred days in a facility.
- Qualified money is at the mercy of the IRS and Congress. They set the guidelines and mandate regulations concerning your retirement plan, including Social Security, Medicare, Medicaid, income tax brackets, required distributions, and estate tax levels. When applying for Medicaid, qualified funds must be spent down to state limits prior to Medicaid assistance.

Qualified Incomes

It is important when planning for retirement to position your assets to work in coordination with your working income. Without proper planning, long-term care issues can be devastating. Social Security and pensions are other forms of qualified money that are not protected from Uncle Sam. Both are incomes and are received regularly. Upon the need for nursing home care, these incomes are automatically taken into consideration and used to pay for care. Social Security, pensions, and qualified funds are self-insuring components. Therefore, they are factored into the equation when being financially evaluated by the Medicaid program in your state.

What happens if you are married? Protecting your assets is twice as important if you are married. Although qualified money is in your name and Social Security number, your assets are combined if your spouse enters a nursing home. Qualified income and assets can be used to help satisfy the cost of nursing home care for your spouse until the assets are spent down to the limits set by the state and federal governments. Imagine needing to enter a long-term care facility for which you had not planned accordingly. What would happen if portions of your incomes were diverted from your spouse?

Case Study 2.1

Several years ago, I met a woman that was very frustrated. She and her husband were retired and on a cruise in the Bahamas when he became dizzy with erratic blood pressure. He had had a small stroke, but it went undiagnosed, and he blamed the illness on the ocean. A few days after they arrived home, he had a major stroke, paralyzing him and sending him into a nursing home.

The couple had worked hard all their lives and were enjoying retirement. They had two homes, a sizable bank account, and qualified plans, but nothing was protected.

By the time the husband passed away, the couple had depleted their bank account and qualified investments to the allowable level before Medicaid stepped in, which at the time was less than one hundred thousand dollars in Massachusetts. Her life was changed forever. In order for the wife to meet her obligations, she had  to sell her cottage to pay the remaining medical bills and create a lifestyle that would fit her new, reduced income.

Fact: *According to ElderLaw Answers in Massachusetts (this may differ per state), Medicaid allows the spouse to maintain a portion of the joint assets, as of 2014, a maximum of $117,240. There is also a limit to the amount of home equity considered as a non-countable asset. Medicaid considers anything above that limit a countable asset.*

There are two viable options to protect these funds:

- legal estate planning documents, designed to protect assets
- an insurance policy designed to fulfill the need for long-term care

In order to protect qualified assets, a legal or insurance program needs to be in place. Otherwise, assets need to be spent down to government limits so the individual will qualify for assistance.

As presented in chapter 1, the federal government has made qualified plans look attractive and beneficial by offering tax considerations. Although these tax considerations appear to be desirable, Uncle Sam has put a price on them, which can outweigh the benefits, reeling you into his domain. Your only option of escape is with the proper protection of your qualified funds with a legal or insurance program.

Irrevocable Retirement Plan Trust

There are two main reasons to use an irrevocable retirement plan trust rather than simply making the retirement plan payable to the surviving spouse. First, for state or federal estate taxes, this would permit the retirement plan to be kept outside the surviving spouse's estate. Second, in the case of second marriages (or spendthrift spouses), this would protect the retirement plan for children and grandchildren. Funds are not placed in the trust until the individual passes away and, therefore, go unprotected and remain vulnerable till death. By using an irrevocable retirement trust, the spouse will not lose the opportunity to utilize the funds.

The trust is the designated beneficiary making the trust a qualified trust by the IRS. The trust is funded with retirement assets and can use the five-million-dollar tax exemption on the first spouse that passes away. The trust is not included in the spouse's estate and may have more favorable calculations when determining required minimum distributions.

Long-term Care Insurance

Long-term care insurance is designed to protect all assets by providing income to the individual to pay for services necessary to perform daily functions. Ultimately, the plan as designed will allow the individual to retain his or her income and assets as if the person did not need care. This in turn allows the individual and spouse to maintain the lifestyle they are accustomed to during this difficult time.

Fact: *According to Employee Benefit Research Institute, "In 2012, only 14% of all individuals older than age 60 have a long term care insurance policy." This means that for 86 percent of all individuals over sixty, if they have assets that are unprotected, they're taking a risk and allowing the cards to land where they may.*

It is advisable to seek professional advice from your estate planning attorney and CPA regarding these matters.

For More Information

Please reference article 1 at the end of the book, "What Few Know about Their 401(k) and Other Qualified Retirement Funds."

CHAPTER 2 REVIEW QUESTIONS

1. What is the main message of this chapter?

   A. Qualified money is no good.
   B. Qualified money is vulnerable and can be used to pay for nursing home care if admitted to a nursing home after the first one hundred days.
   C. Once a person is deceased, his or her qualified money can be protected with an IRS approved trust.
   D. Both B and C.

2. The only program that can protect qualified income and assets from being used in the event you need nursing home care is:

   A. Medicaid.
   B. A long-term care insurance plan.
   C. Medicare.
   D. None of the above.

3. The US government works hard to protect our retirement plans from government intervention for long-term care use.

   TRUE   FALSE

4. Social Security and pensions are considered qualified income; therefore, they are taxable and vulnerable for long-term care prior to Medicaid.

   TRUE   FALSE

Answers: 1. B, 2. B, 3. FALSE, 4. TRUE

CHAPTER 3

Forced to Take Money Out and Forced to Pay Taxes

As presented in chapters 1 and 2, the US government decides the rules and regulations that govern qualified retirement plans since taxes have not been paid on these funds. Since qualified retirement funds must follow the guidelines of qualified plans, you are generally required by the government to begin taking withdrawals from your plans no later than the year you turn 70½. Citizens must take no less than the specified amount based on their age and one of the three Uniform Lifetime Tables (which is based on life expectancy) established by our government. This is called the required minimum distribution, or RMD, and it is 100 percent taxable.

Current Uniform Distribution Table Chart as Found in IRS Publication 590			
Age	Divisor	Age	Divisor
70	27.4	86	14.1
71	26.5	87	13.4
72	25.6	88	12.7
73	24.7	89	12.0
74	23.8	90	11.4
75	22.9	91	10.8
76	22.0	92	10.2
77	21.2	93	9.6
78	20.3	94	9.1
79	19.5	95	8.6
80	18.7	96	8.1
81	17.9	97	7.6
82	17.1	98	7.1
83	16.3	99	6.7
84	15.5	100	6.3
85	14.8	101	5.9

The chart continues to age 115 and the divisor decreases to 1.9.

The above chart is from Table III, the most commonly used table to calculate RMD in IRS Publication 590.

To calculate your RMD:

- Take your age (as of your birthday that tax year) to find your divisor.
- Add the total of all your qualified accounts and divide them by the divisor in the chart.

Example: At age seventy-five, the divisor is currently 22.9. If you have $500,000 in qualified money, that amount divided by the divisor, 22.9, gives your RMD for the year as $21,834.06.

If you take less RMD than the required amount, you will be penalized 50 percent on the amount you failed to take plus interest.

Analyzing RMD and How It Affects Taxability

As you take RMDs, and as time goes on, the divisor gets smaller as in chart 3.1, but your subsequent RMDs may constitute a larger percentage of payout.

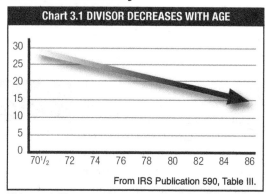

From IRS Publication 590, Table III.

This graph illustrates that as an individual grows older, the divisor gets smaller.

As Chart 3.2 demonstrates, RMD increases due to decreasing divisor.

In this example, the individual took his RMD ($21,834.06, or about 4.37 percent of $500,000) and nothing more. If the remaining principal grows greater than 4.37 percent and the divisor decreases each year, a larger distribution is required.

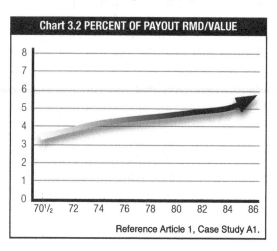

Reference Article 1, Case Study A1.

When adding an inherited qualified plan, which can be very complex, it is advisable to seek the opinion of a professional. The divisor doesn't change, but the RMD may, possibly affecting your income taxes and net amount of your Social Security benefits.

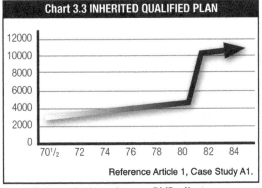

Chart 3.3 INHERITED QUALIFIED PLAN

Reference Article 1, Case Study A1.

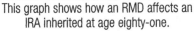

This graph shows how an RMD affects an IRA inherited at age eighty-one.

In this next example, illustrated in chart 3.3, the individual inherited her spouse's qualified plan at age eighty-one. Although she and her husband took their RMDs while both were alive, they benefited by having more deductions and exemptions while filing their taxes as married filing jointly. Chart 3.3 demonstates the RMD of one individual (widowed), now at an older age with a smaller divisor.

Chart 3.3 shows the combined effect of charts 3.1 and 3.2 while adding an inherited qualified plan at age eighty-one. Receiving an inherited qualified plan results from the death of a loved one who has named you as a beneficiary. It creates a change in tax exemptions and deductions. If inherited from a spouse, your tax status changes from married filing jointly to single, which can also change your tax bracket.

When combining these changes, an increasing RMD will:

- make your income increase, which can
- make your taxable income go up, which will
- affect your Social Security, since your qualified income goes up.

Creating a larger taxable event means that you pay more income tax.

Also, the RMD can change as our government sees fit to change tax codes, mandates, guidelines, life-expectancy charts, and the Uniform Lifetime Table.

For More Information

Please reference article 1, "What Few Know about Their 401(k) and Other Qualified Retirement Funds."

CHAPTER 3 REVIEW QUESTIONS

1. What do the initials RMD represent?

    A. Read more daily.
    B. Reserved money for distribution.
    C. Required minimum distribution.
    D. Reverse mortgage discrimination.

2. An RMD is not taxed because the IRS requires money to be withdrawn starting at age 70½.

    TRUE   FALSE

3. The RMD can change the taxability of Social Security benefits.

    TRUE   FALSE

4. Failure to take your entire RMD will result in a 50 percent penalty based on the amount not taken.

    TRUE   FALSE

Answers: 1. C, 2. FALSE, 3. TRUE, 4. TRUE

CHAPTER 4

Social Security Benefits, Concern, and Taxability

Chapter 1 addresses qualified assets. When a qualified asset is distributed, the distribution is recognized and referred to as qualified income. Not to be confused with qualified asset distributions as income, Social Security and pensions are qualified incomes and are also taxable. Many Americans contribute to one or both of these programs and are entitled to receive their benefits, regardless of how they affect their income tax. Generally, Social Security and/or pension strategies are built into their retirement plan as a necessary income and are taxed accordingly. Information previously discussed has a domino effect on your retirement and should be properly coordinated.

Based on the information collected while researching and writing *Positioning 4 Retirement*, it is apparent that the Social Security system in this country is much larger than people realize. Knowing the vast nature of this system, it is incomprehensible to think that Social Security could ever not exist to take care of the American family.

The Social Security program supports individuals who are retired, widowed, married, divorced, or disabled or care for their disabled family member. If the system ever failed, then it would put our economy into a tailspin; homelessness, welfare, crime, and poverty levels would be staggering.

The Social Security Administration has been moving cautiously to trim programs where individuals have found opportunity to capitalize on the system. Research also reveals a need to change the system to fit current and foreseeable concerns. Change can be positive to those who need the system for the reasons that it was designed. For individuals that are legally taking advantage of the system, change will have a negative impact. Unfortunately, there are individuals that are using the system fairly and are caught between the old rules and the new rules.

How Social Security Benefits Are Determined

Social Security retirement benefits are intended for individuals, their spouse, their ex-spouse, or their family members who have paid into the system for at least ten years. Most people file for their benefit when they retire and/or are between ages sixty-two and seventy. There is no advantage to filing after seventy years old.

Benefits are based on

Birth Year	Full Retirement Age
Prior to 1943	65
1943-1954	66
1955	66 + 2 months
1956	66 + 4 months
1957	66 + 6 months
1958	66 + 8 months
1959	66 + 10 months
1960 and later	67

Those with a birthday on January 1 should refer to the preceding year.

a chart that was established by the Social Security Administration.

An individual's benefit is determined by his or her full retirement age that is assigned by the year that he or she was born. The benefit is calculated from a person's highest thirty-five years of earnings. The income a person receives is based on a credit system. Each year after the thirty-fifth year, the system will reject the lowest earnings year and replace it with the new larger one, maintaining the top thirty-five income-earnings years.

Taking Benefits Early or Delaying Benefits

Many people choose to file for their benefit and put it on hold, delaying the income until they are seventy years old—the age when it stops growing—and accumulating an increased benefit. Others choose to begin receiving their benefit earlier than full retirement age—as early as sixty-two years old—and will accept a reduced benefit ranging between 20 and 30 percent.

Birth Year	Full Retirement Age	% of Reduction
Prior to 1937	65	20%
Between 1943 and 1954	66	25%
1960 +	67	30%
Benefits are calculated based on the individual's age. This illustration presents a range of birthdates; not all age groups are presented.		

Knowing how reduced and increased rates are determined is important when electing an early or delayed benefit. The percentages of reduced or increased benefits are based on the individual's date of birth, gender, and one of the many life-expectancy charts created by the government. The current life expectancy chart used for this purpose predicts that a man aged sixty-five years old will live until he is approximately eighty-four, and a woman until she is eighty-six. There is a chance that one out of four people will live to ninety and one of ten will live beyond ninety-five years old.

Based on the chart:

- A person that takes Social Security benefit early could have a longer benefit period. If he or she takes the benefit at sixty-two, then he or she could receive a benefit for twenty-two (male) or twenty-four (female) years.
- The same individual that delays the benefit until seventy years old could have a shorter benefit period of fourteen (male) or sixteen (female) years.

The purpose of a larger benefit is so individuals at age eighty-four/eighty-six will have reached equal benefit, based on their Social Security incomes. The individual that delayed his or her benefit will exceed in overall benefit if he or she lives longer than eighty-four/eighty-six. In order to catch up, the individual who received benefits prior to full retirement age would need to grow his or her benefits 8 percent annually until reaching age seventy.

When Benefits Are Paid

Social Security benefits are paid for the previous month. Benefits are paid one out of four possible days a month, based on the day you were born. Pay dates are the third of each month, as well as on the second, third, or fourth Wednesday of the month.

When an individual passes away, the benefit he or she received for that month must be returned! If a person receives his or her benefit on March 3 and dies on March 30, then the individual will likely receive a benefit on April 3 for the month of March. The benefit collected for the month of passing must be returned to the Social Security Administration.

Upon the death of a spouse, Social Security assigns the larger of the benefits to the surviving spouse. The exception to this rule is if a pension is involved. Social Security will also send the surviving spouse or family member $255 to be applied to burial costs.

Note: *Disabled widows and widowers can receive benefits as early as age fifty and can update their benefit at full retirement age.*

Inflation

Inflation is managed on an annual basis. A cost-of-living increase may be applied once a file is opened, based on the Consumer Pricing Index (CPI) and congressional approval.

How Pensions Work with Social Security Benefits

Single individuals that pay into the Social Security program and work for a company that offers a pension plan can collect 100 percent of each benefit. When married spouses have a combination of pensions and Social Security benefits, it can get a bit confusing upon the death of a spouse. Different from military pensions, government pensions (federal, state, and local) do not contribute to the Social Security system. Individuals that have contributed to both systems may experience a reduced benefit upon retirement.

Upon the death of a spouse when there is a government pension and a Social Security benefit, Social Security will recalculate the surviving spouse's benefit to reflect the combination. Military service members can receive their pension and Social Security benefit. Extra credits are added to members of the military under certain circumstances.

Social Security Taxability

Social Security is considered to be qualified income and can be taxable. An individual's or couple's adjusted gross income determines its taxability. The 2014 threshold and Social Security taxability are as follows:

	Individual	Couples Filing Jointly
Threshold (no tax)	under $25,000	under $32,000
50% Taxability	$25,000–$34,000	$32,000–$44,000
85% Taxability	more than $34,000	more than $44,000

Coordinating this tax element along with other qualified incomes, such as a pension or RMDs from qualified retirement plans, can put a person in a substantial taxable situation. Special incomes, such as bonuses, vacation pay, commissions, and sick pay, that were earned prior to receiving a Social Security benefit may be excluded from the Social Security tax calculation. Pension incomes are 100 percent taxable, regardless!

Taxability and Delaying Social Security

For some individuals, delaying Social Security until age seventy may make sense. Delaying Social Security not only increases the monthly benefit, but it also allows individuals to use their qualified funds first. This eliminates the possibility of two taxable events occurring at the same time. There is approximately a 65 percent increase in benefit when it is taken at age seventy rather than age sixty-two.

Spouse's Benefits

Spouses and qualifying ex-spouses who have never worked or have low earnings may be eligible to receive a benefit of up to 50 percent based on their spouse's or ex-spouse's Social Security benefit. Spouse's benefits and family benefits of Social Security were designed with the stay-at-home spouse in mind. Social Security spousal benefits should be distributed privately; the ex-spouse does not need to know that benefits are being collected—spousal benefits have no effect on the primary earner's benefit.

Suspend and Restrict Spouse's Benefits

To suspend or restrict Social Security benefits involves the use of spouse's benefits. They are two separate actions that allow a spouse to receive a benefit under different circumstances. Only one spouse can take advantage of either one of the added benefits.

To suspend Social Security benefits allows a spouse to receive an additional benefit based on the working spouse's benefit. This opportunity works best with couples when the higher income-earning spouse chooses to work beyond his or her full retirement age, delaying his or her benefit. Suspending allows the younger spouse to file and receive a benefit at age sixty-two with an enhanced benefit. This can only happen after the older working spouse files and suspends his or her benefit at full retirement age. The benefit is based on the elder spouse's benefit at full retirement age. If the younger spouse generated an income and his or her benefit is smaller than 50 percent, then the benefit is adjusted to accommodate the combination of benefits. Once the higher income-earning spouse or elder spouse retires, he or she will receive a benefit based on his or her current age. This opportunity is at its peak when the income-earning spouse is at full retirement age and the other spouse is sixty-two years old. If the income-earning spouse retires at age seventy, then the spouse would receive an additional benefit for up to eight years. Once the elder spouse retires, assuming he or she is seventy years old, the couple would then receive benefits reflecting their ages (sixty-two and seventy).

Restricting an application is a strategy that is used to maximize Social Security benefits for one spouse and to collect a spousal benefit. It generally works best when both spouses are relatively close in age and one is planning to work beyond full retirement age, possibly until age seventy.

Once both spouses have reached full retirement age, one spouse retires and takes his or her benefit while the other spouse continues to work, filing his or her Social Security application as "restricted." This will allow the working spouse to delay his or her benefit and receive a spousal benefit. This strategy does not take away any benefits from the retired spouse. There is a very small window of opportunity for this to take place since full retirement age is between sixty-five and sixty-seven and the maximum benefit is reached at age seventy.

Moving In and Out of the System

Prior to December 8, 2010, the system allowed individuals to file for their benefit at age sixty-two and return it without interest before their seventieth birthday to receive the enhanced benefit. This allowed those who were unsure if they could or wanted to retire to change their mind and reenter the workforce, returning the funds back to the system.

Many people perceived this as an opportunity to take a tax-free loan from the government. When taxability was factored in, it became apparent that what looked like an opportunity was not in many cases.

In 2010, the Social Security Administration published a press release, with changes effective immediately, restricting the timing and limiting the opportunity to extend the benefits. Many individuals found themselves stuck with a Social Security benefit based at an age below seventy.

Weighing the Opportunities

Taxability and change are two risks prevalent when using these strategies. Changes made by the Social Security Administration may be enacted without warning. The financial tax advantage or disadvantage of these changes should be considered. The real risk is the changes that may be coming from the Social Security Administration without notice.

Social Security and Medicare

Social Security and Medicare, although they interact, are separate programs. You do not need to contribute directly to the Social Security system in order to receive Medicare benefits. As a citizen or legal resident of five years or more, an individual can meet Medicare criteria through a spouse or ex-spouse that contributed to the system or paid Medicare payroll taxes; otherwise, premiums are based on the number of credits contributed to Social Security. Medicare eligibility is age sixty-five and has nothing to do with early, full, or delayed retirement ages. It is suggested that individuals enroll in Medicare three months prior to their sixty-fifth birthday, regardless of their retirement plan. Enrollment takes place through the Social Security Administration.

For More Information

Please reference article 2, "Social Security Benefits and Options for Retirement," at the end of the book for more detailed information on this topic.

CHAPTER 4 REVIEW QUESTIONS

1. Social Security retirement benefits can be taken:

    A. As early as sixty-two with a reduced benefit.
    B. Never, or as late as seventy years old with an increased benefit.
    C. At full retirement age.
    D. All of the above.

2. Medicare is available at sixty-five years old, regardless of when Social Security benefits are taken, and individuals are encouraged to enroll at least three months prior to age sixty-five.

    TRUE   FALSE

3. Social Security retirement benefits are an entitlement to all Americans.

    TRUE   FALSE

4. Social Security advises individuals to take their benefits as soon as possible.

    TRUE   FALSE

5. There are risks involved when using the Social Security system for unintended purposes.

    TRUE   FALSE

6. Social Security is taxable up to 85 percent, based on qualified incomes and distributions.

    TRUE   FALSE

Answers: 1. D, 2. TRUE, 3. FALSE, 4. FALSE, 5. TRUE, 6. TRUE

CHAPTER 5

The Effect of Qualified Money on Your Social Security and Taxes

At the beginning of chapter 4, the relationship between qualified distributions and incomes is explained. This chapter discusses qualified incomes, such as Social Security and pensions, and the effect qualified assets have on these incomes. It presents case studies that demonstrate how these incomes and asset  distributions interact regarding taxability during retirement.

At the beginning of each year, we anxiously await the arrival of our tax documents from the previous year. Starting in February, taxpayers meet with their CPAs or tax preparers who organize their clients' taxes, complete forms, and deliver results. In this book, income tax refers to federal income tax, not state income tax.

Income is organized on the first page of our federal tax form. The preparer inputs the data from the tax forms, and the software calculates the adjusted gross income (AGI). In the software that calculates the adjusted gross income, there is a lengthy formula designed to calculate the ratio of qualified money and Social Security benefit. Social Security can be taxable up to 85 percent. Pensions are 100 percent taxable. This does not mean that everyone is going to pay a tax on his or her benefits. The amount of qualified income and assets received will determine the taxability of an individual's or couple's Social Security benefit(s).

It is easier to understand the material in this chapter with the use of examples. The following three case studies show how the taxability of your qualified income affects your Social Security and/or pension benefits.

Case Study 5.1

In this case study, the individual's qualified income is within the parameters necessary to keep the Social Security ratio from increasing. In this case, Social Security is not taxable. Pension and qualified distribution will always be 100 percent. For non-qualified distribution, only the interest is 100 percent taxable.

Annual income was as follows:

	Income	Percent of Income Taxed	Taxable Income
Social Security	$12,000	0%	$0
Pension	$5,000	100%	$5,000
Qualified distribution	$8,733	100%	$8,733
Non-quali-fied distribution	$12,500		$175*
Total	$38,233		$13,908
* Represents the interest earned, which is 100% taxable.			

This client's taxable income of $13,908 is less than his current threshold (per the IRS); therefore, his qualified money is not taxable, and the individual pays minimal federal income tax.

The threshold for taxable income is the line in the sand established by the IRS and is susceptible to change. There are many thresholds established for different situations. Consult your tax advisor about your threshold. Adjusted gross income below this level experiences little to no tax. Income above the threshold is taxable, based on the tax table for that year. Everything is subject to change.

Case Study 5.2

In this case study, the subject received a sizable amount of qualified money (income and assets) from her deceased spouse, which created an adjustment to the Social Security tax formula.

The annual income is as follows:

	Income	Percent of Income Taxed	Taxable Income
Wages	$10,000	100%	$10,000
Social Security	$6,876	85%	$5,845
Pension	$50,000	100%	$50,000
Annuities	$7,871		$1,707*
Qualified RMD	$9,818	100%	$9,818
Total	**$84,565**		**$77,370**
*Represents taxable interest as in case study 5.1.			

The income, along with part-time wages and interest earned, places the individual at a 25 percent tax bracket. After deductions and exemptions, she paid $12,275 in taxes; her effective tax rate ($12,275 divided by $77,370) is 15.87 percent.

This case study has a strong pension (qualified), a Social Security benefit left from a spouse (qualified), and an RMD (qualified), forcing her Social Security formula to adjust based on her AGI (adjusted gross income). Therefore, 85 percent of the Social Security benefit is taxable. The amount of taxable Social Security is $5,845, with an effective tax rate of 15.87 percent, which equals $928 (15.87 percent of $5,845) and goes back to the US Treasury in the form of income tax.

Case Study 5.3

This case illustrates an individual in his seventies that continues to work while collecting Social Security and is forced to take his RMDs. The subject believed in the system and placed 100 percent of his retirement assets in qualified plans with the following results:

	Income	Percent of Income Taxed	Taxable Income
Wages & miscellaneous compensation	$185,670	100%	$185,670
Social Security	$27,582	85%	$23,445
Distribution from Qualified Accounts	$120,675	100%	$120,675
Total	$333,927		$329,790

Case study 5.3 demonstrates the net effect qualified assets create when taken as income:

- The individual is in the 33 percent tax bracket, and after deductions and exemptions, the individual's effective tax rate is 27.18 percent.
- His Social Security is 85 percent taxable.
- The end result is $6,372 ($23,445 x 27.18%) of his Social Security benefit is returned to the US Treasury in the form of income tax.
- His after-tax Social Security income is $21,210 ($27,582 - $6,372).

As in case study 5.2, deductions and exemptions are low creating a larger effective tax rate. The individuals in these three cases more than likely have no mortgage and therefore do not have deductible interest. Their children are on their own, and in these cases, their spouses have passed away minimizing exemptions. This creates their effective tax rate to become greater, which creates larger taxability.

Had the subjects only matched their employers' contributions to a qualified plan and put the remaining contributions in a Roth or a non-qualified retirement plan, then they would have had a lower effective tax rate. The subjects would not have had to pay as much tax. In this situation, knowing the strength of the qualified incomes, which are predictable, it would have been better if the individuals had accumulated non-qualified assets instead of qualified ones. (Roth and non-qualified funds are discussed further on.)

For More Information

Please reference articles 1 and 2, "What Few Know about Their 401(k) and Other Qualified Retirement Funds" and "Social Security Benefits and Options for Retirement," respectively, at the end of this book for more detailed infomation.

CHAPTER 5 REVIEW QUESTIONS

1. Social Security is an entitlement and is therefore not taxable.

    TRUE   FALSE

2. Money taken out of a qualified retirement plan can affect the taxability of Social Security benefits.

    TRUE   FALSE

3. Qualified money can put people in a greater tax bracket.

    TRUE   FALSE

4. Qualified funds that fall under the RMD rule are not taxable.

    TRUE   FALSE

Answers: 1. FALSE, 2. TRUE, 3. TRUE, 4. FALSE

Who Has Control of Your Retirement Funds: You or the Government?

After reading chapters 1 through 5, you might be getting the feeling that you have lost control over your qualified retirement plans. The truth is you never had control over your qualified plans, even though you were led to believe otherwise.

The psychology behind Black Friday is the same strategy that is used with qualified money. Like shoppers panicking to find the perfect deal, people add to their qualified funds as if it is an addiction. Offering a product at a perceived advantage and limiting the amount and time period to acquire the item make us rush in and grab as much as we can. Here is how qualified money relates:

- Some employers match qualified funds (free money).
- Qualified funds then grow tax deferred (added advantage).
- Accumulation limits are set (create anxiety, greed, and false need).
- Upon distribution, pay tax at a potentially lower tax rate (more for less).
- Then place requirements on the opportunity (it must be good).

Not only do people jump at the opportunity, but they also contribute as much as they can, putting more and more money into a qualified position until they reach the limit the government has set.

What you have control over is the role that qualified money plays in the overall plan. By understanding how qualified money works and who controls the rules for qualified money, individuals can make it work to their advantage.

Understand that qualified money is controlled by the US government with guidelines, mandates, laws, and rules that can and do change to meet the needs of the country. It is important to understand that large corporations drive Congress and have influence in developing these mandates, guidelines, laws, and rules.

Qualified money should be used to supplement Social Security and/or pensions that fall under similar limitations. Qualified money should not be accumulated to be used for large purchases because it will create greater taxability.

Now that you know the position qualified money plays in your retirement years, planning becomes imperative.

For More Information

Please reference article 1, "What Few Know about Their 401(k) and Other Qualified Retirement Funds," at the end of this book for more detailed information.

CHAPTER 6 REVIEW QUESTIONS

1. Ultimately, what organization controls qualified money by setting the limitations and guidelines for it?

    A. The US government.
    B. The IRS.
    C. Congress.
    D. All of the above.

2. Big businesses have no control over the decisions that are made regarding qualified retirement plans.

    TRUE   FALSE

3. Qualified money should be coordinated to supplement Social Security and pensions.

    TRUE   FALSE

Answers: 1. D, 2. FALSE, 3. TRUE

Practical Application I

Identifying Your Personal Qualified Incomes and Assets and Applying Them to Your Retirement Perspective

Now that we have identified qualified money, let's put it into perspective in relation to your personal situation by answering the following questions.

1. **Approximately what will your Social Security benefit be if you retire at age sixty-two, full retirement age, or seventy?**

    - Visit the Retirement Estimator at www.ssa.gov to determine your benefit for these ages if you don't have your annual Social Security statement.
    - If you are receiving your Social Security, you can visit the same site. Go to "my Social Security" for a record of your benefit history.
    - Visit **www.Positioning4Retirement.com**, print out and complete worksheet (WS):

        WS 1   Qualified Income from Social Security

2. **Do you have one or more pensions? If yes, what will the monthly benefit be when you choose to take it/them?**

    - To analyze your pension, go to **www.Positioning4Retirement.com** and print out and complete:

        WS 2   Qualified Income from Pensions

3. **How much qualified money (assets) have you accumulated?**

    - To assist you in answering this question, the following worksheets on the website, **www.Positioning4Retirement.com**, will help you organize your funds so you can track them. Print only the ones that pertain to you.

        WS 8   Qualified Employer-sponsored Plans
        WS 9   Qualified IRA Certificate of Deposit (CD) Accounts
        WS 10   Qualified Annuities (IRA)
        WS 11   Qualified Brokerage Accounts

4. Transfer the information from the worksheets you completed for questions 1, 2, and 3, above, to the spreadsheet, also found on www.Positioning4Retirement.com.

If at anytime assistance is needed, contact the Retirement Education Resource Center of North America, Inc. at 781-763-RERC (7372) or email us at help@ positioning4retirement.com.

What This Information Represents

- Question 1 represents the fixed income you receive. Taxability is based on how much qualified money you take each year from question 3.
- Question 2 deals with funds that are completely taxable and likely to affect the taxability of your Social Security benefit.
- Question 3 represents the qualified asset(s) that you will pay taxes on based on the amount of total qualified money you take as income in any given year.

Other questions you may want to ask in order to receive advice on how you can lower your incomes tax are the following:

1. What are your current tax bracket and your effective tax rates (income tax paid divided by adjusted gross earnings)?
2. If you are receiving Social Security, how much is currently taxable?

Getting to Know Your Non-qualified Retirement Plan

CHAPTER 7

The Opposite of North Is South—Two Distinct Directions

Chapters 1 through 6 address the first step toward understanding qualified assets and incomes in a retirement plan. The second step is understanding the role of non-qualified money. The opposite of qualified money is non-qualified money. Non-qualified money has the following advantages over qualified money:

- A tax has already been paid on the non-qualified money.
- There are more options for protecting assets from extended care/long-term care needs.
- It can have its own identification number.
- There are no government requirements as to when you can use it.
- You can use as much or as little as you want.
- It can grow tax deferred with fewer limitations in the correct program.

We use non-qualified money to buy groceries, pay the mortgage, pay our monthly bills, go on vacation, buy gifts, and save for retirement. Non-qualified money is the money in your:

- checkbook
- savings account
- savings bonds
- cash-value life insurance
- non-qualified annuities
- CDs that are not IRA CDs
- stocks, bonds, mutual funds, etc.

Cash value life insurance and non-qualified annuities grow tax deferred, unlike investments that are taxed annually.

The major differences in what non-qualified retirement funds provide, compared to qualified ones, are the following:

- Non-qualified retirement funds have the ability to accumulate without limitations or restrictions and supplement Social Security without major tax consequences (as seen in case study 5.1).
- Generally, the principal will have no effect on Social Security. (Large withdrawals can create capital gains and large interest earnings, which could cause a negative effect. Consulting a CPA is advised.)
- Non-qualified retirement funds provide protection for your family with legal documents and the ability to meet extended care/long-term care objectives. Most important, this money belongs to you, and Uncle Sam does not have access to it if properly positioned.

Non-qualified funds are vulnerable to Medicaid, as are all assets if not protected. Non-qualified funds are easier to protect from long-term care needs since they represent everyday cash on hand and can be assigned to a trust with its own tax identification number.

A Chart Is Worth a Thousand Words

The following chart illustrates types of funds and whether or not they can be considered qualified. As you will note, many types can be partly or fully positioned as qualified and/or non-qualified.

Type of Fund	Qualified	Non-qualified
Cash		X
Savings		X
Checking		X
CDs	X	X
Stocks	X	X
Bonds	X	X
Mutual Funds	X	X
Hedge Funds	X	X
Annuities	X	X

There are twice as many opportunities for placing funds in a non-qualified position as in a qualified position.

Why don't more people coordinate their qualified and non-qualified funds better? Here are the main reasons.

- They may not be aware of the consequences qualified money imposes.
- They may not be aware of other opportunities.
- They may be too busy and overwhelmed with professional/family responsibilities, and retirement planning may not be on their radar.
- They may not understand the importance of coordinating qualified and non-qualified money.
- They may be getting the wrong advice from friends and family.
- Their advisor may be uninformed of the need to position assets.

It is important to have all the information. Be aware of your own circumstances and consult with your team of professionals.

For More Information

Please reference article 1, "What Few Know about Their 401(k) and Other Retirement Funds."

CHAPTER 7 REVIEW QUESTIONS

1. What is non-qualified money?

   A. Money that I contribute to my retirement from my paycheck that my employer matches.
   B. Money that has not been taxed yet.
   C. The opposite of qualified money; money that has already been taxed.
   D. None of the above.

2. What makes money non-qualified in the retirement sense?

   A. It has been taxed.
   B. It has not been taxed.
   C. It can't grow tax deferred.

3. If unprotected, non-qualified assets can be absorbed by Medicaid.

   TRUE   FALSE

Practical Application II
Identifying Your Personal Non-qualified Money and Applying It to Your Retirement Perspective

Now that we have identified non-qualified money, let's put it into perspective in relation to your personal situation by completing the following exercises.

1. Do you have any non-qualified assets? If so, list each with its value.

For your convenience and to make the task of organizing easy, gather the information and complete the following worksheets (WS) found on the website, **www.Positioning4Retirement.com**.

Again, print out only the ones you need.

WS 14 Non-qualified Assets – Checking Account
WS 15 Non-qualified Assets – Savings Accounts
WS 16 Non-qualified Assets – Savings Bonds
WS 17 Non-qualified Assets – Money Market Accounts
WS 18 Non-qualified Certificates of Deposit
WS 19 Non-qualified Annuities
WS 20 Non-qualified Brokerage Accounts

If at anytime assistance is needed, contact the Retirement Education Resource Center of North America, Inc. at 781-763-RERC (7372) or email us at help@ positioning4retirement.com.

2. Once completed, move the requested information to the spreadsheet found on the website.

What This Information Represents

Your total of non-qualified assets represents funds that have been taxed and are available to you prior to retirement.

THE EXCEPTION
TO THE RULE

CHAPTER 8

Roth Plans
The Hidden Treasure

In order to understand a Roth plan, it is best to first understand the difference between qualified and non-qualified funds. Now that you have an understanding and know the differences between qualified and non-qualified money, let's discuss Roth plans.

A Roth is a qualified plan that accepts only non-qualified funds. Non-qualified funds upon entering a Roth plan become qualified and follow the rules and regulations imposed on qualified funds with a few differences as presented in this chapter.

Remember the Black Friday analogy in chapter 6? Using the same tactic, Roth plans are a way for the US government to offer those with moderate incomes an opportunity to balance out the tax consequences of qualified money, understanding that our society is not aware of the dangers of qualified funds.

As with qualified plans, a person must follow guidelines for qualified money and additionally meet the following criteria when opening a Roth plan:

- The individual must be employed and show proof of income earned by presenting a W-2 or Form 1099 at tax time. Although this is evident with an employer-sponsored plan, it is not evident with a Roth IRA.

- The person must make less than the allowable limits. If he or she makes more than the allowable limit, then he or she must calculate his or her contributions based on an IRS worksheet to avoid paying a 6 percent excise tax on the overfunded portion of the contribution.
- The individual must keep the initial funds in the account for at least five years without any withdrawals in order to receive the benefits of a Roth account. Subsequent contributions are considered part of the initial deposit.
- Personal contributions cannot exceed the allowable limits based on the plan in a given year and the individual's age.

There are two types of Roth plans:

- A **designated Roth account** is an employer-sponsored plan that is controlled by the employer.
- A **Roth IRA** is an individual account offered by banks, insurance companies, and investment companies.

The difference between a designated Roth account and a Roth IRA are as follows. Designated Roth accounts are offered by the employer, but not all employers offer a Roth option in their sponsored programs. Funds can accept contributions up to the qualified limits ($17,500 in 2014). Plus, if the individual is fifty years old and employed, then he or she can contribute an additional limit annually ($5,500 in 2014) until age 70½, which is when the person has to begin withdrawing from the account. Withdrawing from a designated Roth account can make up all or part of your RMD. If entirely liquidated and the account experiences an overall loss, the loss is tax deductible, subject to certain limitations. Contributions stop once you retire, if prior to age 70½.

A Roth IRA is independent from employer-sponsored plans. Unlike a designated Roth, a Roth IRA does not contribute to your RMD calculation. Contributions into a Roth IRA can continue after age 70½. Contribution limits are currently $5,500 annually for people forty-nine and younger and $6,500 annually for people age fifty and older. This additional $1,000 is often referred to as a catch-up contribution.

The two types of Roth plans have the following in common.

- All funds that enter into it are non-qualified; the funds have already been taxed. The funds are going to become qualified when they go into the Roth plan.

- Funds must remain in the individual's name and Social Security number. Even though they are not taxable, they can be applied to nursing home costs because they are now considered qualified.
- The individual or individuals as a married couple or filing separately—determined by how they file taxes—must keep their income within the guidelines. Currently (in 2014), individual income cannot exceed $114,000, and a married couple must make less than $181,000 filing jointly. Please reference IRS Publication 590 for in-depth, up-to-date information and modified calculation assistance.
- Individuals and married couples that exceed the income guidelines—earning between $114,000 and $129,000 for single individuals and $181,000 and $191,000 for married couples—can still contribute to the plan but must complete IRS Publication 590, worksheet 2-2, which will calculate the allowable contributions.
- Contributions that exceed the allowable limit will receive a 6 percent excise tax.
- The funds grow tax free and are tax free upon withdrawal, provided they are in the plan for five years.
- The funds have to follow the 59½ IRS rule, which carries a 10 percent penalty for withdrawals prior to age 59½ (unless the withdrawal falls under one of the special circumstances).
- When an individual is older than 59½ and the funds have been held in a Roth for over five years, the money can be withdrawn and put back into a non-qualified status.

The benefits of a Roth plan are the following:

- The funds grow tax free.
- Funds withdrawn after age 59½ that have been in the plan for five years are tax free.
- Funds withdrawn can be coordinated with qualified funds in order to offset income tax that is created by the RMD and other qualified fund withdrawals.
- A designated Roth account can contribute to a person's annual RMD while offsetting the taxability of other qualified funds.
- By coordinating a Roth plan with qualified funds, Social Security taxability is manageable, allowing the individual to prevent Social Security benefits from being taxed.

Here is the best part!

You are able to have both plans and have them work independently of each other.

Therefore, by meeting the criteria stated above, individuals have the potential to contribute to the maximum allowable limit on a designated Roth account ($17,500/$23,000) AND contribute to the limit of a Roth IRA ($5,500/$6,500) separately. **This is a twist that allows individuals to help offset the damage that qualified plans can do to taxability and Social Security benefits.**

Before jumping into a Roth or any financial plan, understand that everyone's situation is different. Therefore, it is important to consult your team of professionals to review your options, and they will advise you accordingly.

For More Information

Please reference article 3, "Roth Plans," at the end of the book for more details and examples of how Roth plans work and interact with your retirement planning.

CHAPTER 8 REVIEW QUESTIONS

1. Roth plans accept funds after being taxed and convert them to qualified funds, even though tax has been paid on those funds.

   TRUE   FALSE

2. The two types of Roth Plans are:

   A. Designer Roth accounts and Roth IRSs.
   B. Roth IRAs and designated Roth accounts.

3. RMDs are different between Roth plans.

   TRUE   FALSE

4. Roth plans have additional qualifying criteria along with the criteria of qualified plans.

   TRUE   FALSE

5. Roth plans can help offset taxation that qualified plans create.

   TRUE   FALSE

6. You cannot have more than one Roth plan.

   TRUE   FALSE

Answers: 1. TRUE, 2. B, 3. TRUE, 4. TRUE, 5. TRUE, 6. FALSE

CHAPTER 9

Roth Conversion and Its Loopholes for High-income Earners

A Roth conversion is the process of turning a qualified plan or traditional IRA into a Roth IRA. There are two components involved in a Roth conversion. First, you need a qualified plan or an IRA as presented in chapter 1. Second, you must pay tax on the funds you are converting. If you are converting directly from a qualified plan such as a 401(k), you must have left your employer or be 59½ years old to conduct an in-service distribution. IRAs have no restrictions on how and when you can convert to a Roth. Many people do this to experience the benefits of a Roth IRA.

Prior to 2010, convertibility was limited based on the income cap at $100,000. As of 2010, the convertibility requirements of a qualified IRA to a Roth IRA were eliminated, regardless of income level.

When Is a Good Time to Convert a Traditional IRA to a Roth IRA?

A Roth conversion can take place anytime, and there are no limits on the number of times a person can convert a qualified plan or traditional IRA to a

Roth IRA. Since tax is a consideration, the time to convert funds may be when taxability is low. The best time to convert could be the year of retirement or the following year. Consult your tax advisor to determine the best time to convert.

For example: A couple earned $125,000 annually while employed and has accumulated $150,000 ($100,000 in principal and $50,000 interest earned, pre-tax) in a qualified plan. They retire at the end of the year. The following year, they anticipate earnings from Social Security of $35,000.

Their strategy is as follows:

- They are going to lie low for a year or two, not creating a strong taxable income, living on their Social Security, and withdrawing from non-qualified savings to meet their obligations. They estimate their obligations to be $50,000 annually.
- For the next two years, they will convert part of their qualified plan to a Roth IRA while their income is low, capturing the interest growth that the funds experienced while qualified and taxed at a controlled tax rate during retirement. With the help of their CPA, they decide to convert $30,000 annually creating a taxable income of $65,000 and minimizing the taxability of the funds that are being converted.
- After two years, they will have $60,000 in a Roth, which must remain there for five years before they can use it. They may open separate plans with their own five-year waiting period because they are older than 59½.
- They will then draw off their qualified funds as needed, coordinating the qualified withdrawals and minimizing their tax rate according to the income threshold for that year.
- After five years, they can then begin to access their Roth IRA and continue to convert the remaining qualified funds to a Roth IRA, minimizing their tax exposure while capturing their earned interest.

This method is low risk and is a strategy of coordinating qualified income with non-qualified assets to allow convertibility of a qualified plan or traditional IRA to a Roth IRA.

Roth Convertibility for High-income Earners

Through the process of converting a qualified IRA to a Roth IRA utilizing the conversion process, an individual that earns more than the set income level can establish a Roth IRA; however, there is an IRS risk.

The following tactic creates an opportunity of risk while converting a qualified IRA to a Roth IRA for working individuals and couples, generating an income above the allowable limits.

The process has three steps:

1. Establish a qualified IRA with a financial institution, such as a bank, insurance company, or investment company.
2. Contribute into the qualified IRA for a period of time.
3. Convert the qualified IRA to a Roth IRA. The number of conversions is unlimited; therefore, you can convert as often as you want. However, the IRS may become sensitive if you convert too frequently. They may enact the step transaction doctrine (definition and explanation follow).

Although tax must be paid on the funds when converting a qualified IRA to a Roth, the amount should be small because the tax was from a short period of time. Since both types of IRAs are qualified plans, there is no premature withdrawal penalty.

The step transaction doctrine presents a risk to funds that meet one or more of three criteria—the binding commitment test, mutual interdependence test, and intent test—as explained here. Although the step transaction doctrine is not often seen in this arena, it is a potential threat. The doctrine examines the process of the transaction to determine if there is an underlying means that is being conducted to avoid paying a tax. The first two steps, the binding commitment and the mutual independent tests are generally excused; however, the risk arises with the third step, the intent test. The intent test is focused on the end result and questions the timeliness between events and the independence and purpose of the step. If one step appears to be necessary to accomplish the next step, then the two steps may be considered linked. This test is more subjective than the mutual interdependence test. This is why financial experts suggest that conversions take place at least a year apart. The risk is if the transaction fails the tests then tax, penalties, and fines will be assessed.

What are the benefits of converting to a Roth IRA?

- Once in a Roth, the funds grow tax free.
- Withdrawals are tax free within the qualified guidelines.
- After five years, a Roth can easily be positioned into a non-qualified status.
- A Roth can be coordinated with other tax liabilities, minimizing taxability.

This is an opportunity for high-income earning individuals to utilize Roth IRAs and reap their benefits. Do the benefits outweigh the risks? Maybe.

It is suggested that decisions pertaining to Roth conversions be reviewed by a CPA and attorney.

Employer-sponsored Plans

Notice that the information presented above is based on Roth IRAs, which are independent from employer-sponsored retirement plans. Employer sponsored retirement plans may have triggers within the guidelines of their plans that allow Roth conversions to take place or allow for the individual to remove funds from the employer-sponsored plan. The trigger is generally in the summary plan description of the employer's guidelines, referred to as the "non-hardship withdrawal provision." This allows individuals that are 59½ or older to withdraw qualified funds as a non-hardship rollover. The rollover takes place with the plan administrator's supervision and must involve a trustee-to-trustee rollover, never touching the individual.

There are also triggers in some employer-sponsored plans that allow individuals younger than 59½ to withdraw qualified funds. These elements are established by the plan administrators and are not often presented to the employee because they create unwanted work for the employer. Meeting with the human resources department to explore this opportunity may be advantageous.

It is advised that technical advisors such as a CPA and investment counselors be involved with Roth conversions to avoid the step transaction doctrine.

For More Information

Please reference article 3, "Roth Plans," at the end of this book for more details and examples of how conversions of Roth plans work and interact with your retirement planning.

CHAPTER 9 REVIEW QUESTIONS

1. The best time to convert a qualified IRA to a Roth IRA is when taxable income is low.

    TRUE   FALSE

2. When converting qualified money to a Roth, the qualified money is taxed, even though a Roth is considered qualified.

    TRUE   FALSE

3. The method of converting a qualified IRA to a Roth IRA for high-income earners above the limit has a risk of being reviewed by the IRS in reference to the step transaction doctrine.

    TRUE   FALSE

Answers: 1. TRUE, 2. TRUE, 3. TRUE

Practical Application III
Identifying Your Roth Accounts

Now that we have identified Roth plans, let's put them into perspective in relation to your personal situation by answering the following questions.

Do you have a Roth account through your employer or independently? If so, what are the values?

Using the following worksheets (WS) located at **www.Positioning4Retirement. com**, document your findings for your records and for tracking purposes.

> WS 12 Employer-sponsored (Designated) Roth Accounts
> WS 13 Roth IRA Accounts

Once the worksheet is complete, move the information as directed to the spreadsheet. The spreadsheet will help you track your funds as they grow.

If at anytime assistance is needed, contact the Retirement Education Resource Center of North America, Inc. at 781-763-RERC (7372) or email us at help@ positioning4retirement.com.

What This Information Represents

These amounts represent your retirement accounts that will never be taxed and are available after age 59½, provided the initial deposit has been in the account for five years. Here is the ongoing question presented by the practical application sections of this book:

What can you do to reduce your tax exposure and retain income and assets?

Completing the worksheets and transferring the relevant information to the spreadsheet will help you answer this question. Then also consider the following questions.

- In your opinion, are your qualified and non-qualified plans well-coordinated? Or, do you feel you have too many qualified assets or too few, based on what you have read and the information you have compiled?
- When you retire, will you have enough non-qualified funds to offset the tax damage qualified funds can cause?

- In your estimation, what will be your cost and consequences of collecting qualified assets?

Information will be presented as you read further that will assist you to answer these questions.

Programs Used to Balance and Offset Taxability during Retirement

CHAPTER 10

Measuring the Risk of Coordinating Qualified and Non-qualified Funds

Now that you have an understanding of qualified and non-qualified funds and how they can affect your overall retirement plan, the following suggestions should not be shocking to you.

First, employer-matched retirement funds are always beneficial to the accumulation of your wealth. If the employer offers a designated Roth account, then he or she is giving you another opportunity to maximize your retirement accumulation. Keep in mind that individuals can have a private Roth and an employer-sponsored Roth account. Opening a separate Roth IRA with the bank, your insurance company, or investment companies is also recommended.

Before contributing above your employer match, seek the advice of your professional team. Consulting with your investment and insurance professionals is beneficial because they may have different ideas and, therefore, offer different types of plans to maximize your potential. They may have strong opinions, but you have the ultimate decision.

Also, coordinating qualified and non-qualified programs is essential to controlling tax liability. Keep in mind when discussing options with your team that Roth plans and non-qualified programs, such as cash value life insurance and annuities, should be coordinated with investment programs.

Managing risks when planning your retirement is essential to navigating through a bad market. Among the beginning steps of building a retirement portfolio is securing a disability insurance policy to create an income to include retirement funding. This will help alleviate the risk of losing what has been built in your portfolio because disabilities can drain retirement funds. In the past, disability plans covered income replacement for living expenses and ignored retirement accumulation. Once the disabled person reached retirement age, he or she relied on Social Security for support since the individual's retirement portfolio was absorbed due to the disability. Now, separately or inclusive, disability plans can be written to accommodate retirement portfolios so the disabled individual doesn't have to rely entirely on Social Security. Similar plans cover business loss due to disability as well as other situations.

Addressing Inflation

Oftentimes CDs and EE bonds are used as a safety net, either in a difficult economy or for someone who wants to eliminate risk at all times and at all cost. CDs and savings bonds grow at a minimal rate and often below the inflation rate. The risk is eliminated, as is growth.

For example, assume the inflation rate is 3 percent. If the CD performs less than the inflation rate, it costs you money. A $10,000 CD that grows 1 percent annually is worth $9,800 at the end of the first year, after inflation; you have lost 2 percent (or $200) to inflation. After three years, the same CD is worth $9,049 of purchase power from its inception. Simply, under these conditions, a dollar today will buy approximately 90.5 cents of food, clothing, and necessities in three years. If the dollar you are investing isn't growing greater than inflation, then the same is happening—you are losing some of your investment to inflation.

A solution to this is a short-term fixed annuity. Some annuities work as a CD but offer above-inflation rates. A CD is the same, but it also needs to be rolled over at maturity.

Calculating Risk Exposure

Many attorneys, CPAs, and financial professionals may mention the Rule of 100 as a barometer when considering risk exposure. This rule separates risk from protection. Age determines the recommended amount of funds open to market risk and the amount of funds protected from market vulnerability and volatility. This is when funds move from the investment side of a portfolio to the insurance side.

The Rule of 100

The number 100 minus your age equals the percent of funds suggested to be in a position of risk, vulnerability, and volatility. Age equals the percentage of value to be protected.

100 - Your Age = Percent of Funds Suggested to Be at Risk

Simply put, your age represents the percentage of funds that should be protected from market risk. As you get older, there should be less market risk.

If this rule is followed closely during an economic crisis, then the fallout will not be as devastating.

The Rule of 100 through the Eyes of an Investment Professional

Market value can increase or decrease based on political, economic, and market risk. Risk helps keep up with inflation. The asset classes at risk are variable annuities, stocks, certain bonds, mutual funds, and exchange traded funds (ETFs).

During a meeting with an investment professional, Vincent Serratore, he showed me what he called a "reality check."

He asked if I know 30 + 43 = 0.

So I took the bait and said no.

He explained that if an investment drops 30 percent in one year, it takes about a 43 percent return the following year in order to reach its initial value. Here is an example.

- Year 1 $100,000 investment drops 30 percent ($30,000); its value is now $70,000.
- Year 2 $70,000 grows 43 percent ($30,100); its value is now $100,100 (this example does not take into consideration broker fees and inflation).

Vincent indicated how this example is similar to what we've seen recently. Six times in the last twenty years, the market has been down: 1994, 2000, 2001, 2002, 2008, and 2011. The S&P 500 was up 700 points from 2004 to 2013. In 2002, the market dropped 23.37 percent and rebounded 26 percent in 2003. Market volatility was all over the place while inflation continued to average 3 percent annually.

The rule of 100 helps create a necessary balance, offsetting risk while staying above inflation if you understand that risk is used to keep your portfolio above inflation. A fifty-year-old with 50 percent at risk and 50 percent in a low- to zero-risk portfolio may not do as well overall in a bull market but will breathe easier in a down market.

For More Information

Please reference article 4, "Disability and Your Retirement," at the end of this book for more details and examples of how disability plans work and interact with your retirement planning.

CHAPTER 10 REVIEW QUESTIONS

1. It is suggested that when accumulating qualified funds, a person should only accumulate based on the employer's matching funds.

    TRUE   FALSE

2. If the employer offers a designated Roth account, the employee should utilize the opportunity.

    TRUE   FALSE

3. Coordinating qualified with non-qualified plans is not recommended to control tax liability.

    TRUE   FALSE

4. Disability insurance can now be written to accommodate retirement accumulation.

    TRUE   FALSE

5. The theory behind the Rule of 100 is to diversify the risk of an investment portfolio with safe, low-risk opportunities as you grow older.

    TRUE   FALSE

Answers: 1. TRUE, 2. TRUE, 3. FALSE, 4. TRUE, 5. TRUE

Balance Qualified Funds with Non-qualified Annuities

After examining the pros and cons of qualified funds, the next subject to consider is non-qualified options. Beyond funds that are invested in CDs, stocks, and bonds, there are two types of non-qualified funds that are important to understand: annuities and cash-value/permanent life insurance. Both non-qualified annuities and permanent life insurance policies can play a major role when balancing a retirement plan. Balancing qualified with non-qualified programs helps to avoid unnecessary taxation.

The Role of Annuities in a Retirement Plan

An annuity is an insurance contract that is designed to make scheduled income payments in return for a previously paid premium. Annuities are the only financial tool (outside Social Security and pensions) that will guarantee income for a person's lifetime. Annuities can be qualified or non-qualified.

Non-qualified annuities can be structured as immediate, variable, fixed, or fixed index.

- **Immediate annuities** begin to pay out income either immediately or within the first year of the contract. Since they are being annuitized immediately, there is no surrender period. Based on the terms of the contract, income will continue to pay out for life or a predetermined period of time until the annuity is exhausted or the individual listed as the annuitant dies. Immediate annuities guarantee a risk-free income.

- **Variable annuities** are subject to positive and negative markets. Funds are typically invested in money market funds using stocks, bonds, money market instruments, or a combination of the three.
- **Fixed annuities** are contracts that perform in a predetermined manner providing guaranteed growth and cannot experience losses. They are often used as an alternative to bank CDs.
- **Fixed index annuities** have no market risk since they are fixed programs. Additionally, fixed index annuities offer guaranteed conservative to moderate growth linked to the equity of the indexes. Funds are not invested in the open markets but are invested in the insurance company's portfolio.

Each of these annuities has a place in the market and may have a place in your retirement portfolio. It is not unusual to combine all four types of annuities into one portfolio.

Annuities have the following in common:

- All annuities are insurance products that follow guidelines specific to the state you live in.
- All annuities are backed by the financial integrity of the insurance company.

- All annuities (except for immediate) have surrender periods. It is the insurance company's objective to invest your funds over an extended period to provide the guarantees that they offer. Surrender periods assure the insurance company that they will have funds available.
- All annuities have a "free look period," which provides a time for you to review the contract. If you choose not to keep the contract, then the insurance company will return your funds without penalty.
- All annuities (except immediate annuities) follow the 59½ IRS rule.
- All non-qualified annuities are after-tax funds; the gains are the only taxable portion.
- All annuities grow tax deferred. With a non-qualified annuity, the premium is taxed prior to being placed in the annuity. Once in the annuity, the funds grow tax deferred as they would in a traditional retirement account. Additionally, the funds do not follow the guidelines a traditional retirement account is forced to follow. Once the interest is paid out and taxed, the principal is tax free since it has already been taxed.

Terms to Know and Understand

- **Surrender charge period and penalty.** As mentioned, unique to any other financial product, annuities (with the exception of immediate annuities) have a surrender charge period. During this period, if funds are withdrawn beyond the limits of the penalty-free amount, a surrender charge is applied to the contract. The surrender charge schedule should be reviewed and is fully disclosed.
- **Penalty-free withdrawal allowance.** Generally after the first year, a predetermined percentage of the funds can be withdrawn without a surrender penalty. However, if you are younger than 59½, it does not eliminate the IRS penalty. Not all contracts offer penalty-free withdrawal allowances.
- **Annuitization.** This is when the owner of the contract decides to turn his or her annuity (asset) into income. When this takes place, the annuity is no longer considered an asset. This is an irreversible decision and is often used when planning for Medicaid. Incomes are based on the life expectancy chart, the age and gender of the insured, as well as the value of the annuity at that time. Incomes can be established to last from five years to the lifetime of the insured who is referred to as the annuitant.
- **Income rider.** This is a lifetime systematic withdrawal program to a new contract holder. Although there is generally a cost for the rider, income riders are a great tool for creating an income stream for life as

a supplement to your Social Security or pension without annuitizing the contract. The insurance company guarantees a specific interest growth as a separate pool of money that mirrors and is attached to the annuity. These funds are used strictly for creating an income stream for life. This pool of money works off the value of the annuity. Even if the value of the annuity runs out, the income still continues until the death of the insured.

- **Systematic withdrawals.** This allows the owner of the annuity to withdraw funds on a regularly scheduled basis. Oftentimes this is seen on annuities that were established prior to when income riders came out. The amount is set by the owner of the contract, and it is not an income stream for life. When the funds in the annuity are exhausted, the contract is closed.

- **Bonus.** Many annuities have bonuses that are often considered upfront interest growth. The bonus is an added value to the principal at a predetermined time within the surrender period and becomes part of the contract value during or at the end of the contract.

- **Cap.** Some annuities place an upper limit potential, or cap, on earning potential. If the cap is 5 percent and the growth is 10 percent, then the cap limits the growth to 5 percent.

- **Spread, Margin, and Administration Fees.** These are terms that are used to represent costs that are applied to the contract by subtracting a percentage of growth. Since fixed annuities never lose money, there is no cost applied to the contract in a negative market, except the cost of a rider. A spread, margin, or administration fee generally applies when a contract earns interest.

- **Participation Rate.** All index annuities have a participation rate. The participation rate is the percentage of the index value that will be applied to the contract. For example, if the index growth is 10 percent and the participation rate is 50 percent, then the contract would receive 5 percent of the gain.

- **Crediting Method.** This pertains to fixed index annuities. A crediting method is a measuring tool used by insurance companies to calculate and distribute the insurance company's portfolio growth into the annuity contract. Funds are directly invested in the insurance company's portfolio, not the open market. Crediting methods are generally based on the equity growth of one of the indexes, such as the S&P 500. A popular crediting method is the annual point-to-point method. This method is plugged into an equation that calculates the equity growth from year to year and applies that growth to the contract. The first part of the equation is the result of the crediting method, which will determine contract growth.

- **Annual Reset.** Upon the contract anniversary, gains on the contract lock in and become part of the accumulated value of the contract.
- **Downside Protection.** This is an element found in a fixed and fixed-index annuity that provides guaranteed protection from losses.

Never Run Out of Money

The biggest concern most retirees have today is running out of money. The threats of changes in Social Security and weakened retirement funds from a volatile market have forced people to acknowledge this problem.

Although annuities can be annuitized (how the annuity pays out) using a lifetime income-stream approach, insurance companies have progressed by offering an income rider as described above. An income rider can be added to the annuity upon inception. The income rider generally carries a cost and can be dropped at any time. It offers many advantages when compared to annuitizing.

- Annuitizing is permanent, whereas an income rider can start and stop.
- Guaranteed growth rates independent from the growth methods of the annuity allow the annuity to continue on the same growth path minus any payouts from the rider.
- Additional withdrawals can be taken above and beyond the established income stream. The income stream will adjust, based on the withdrawal.
- Income can be turned on and off as desired, although the rider's growth is generally not turned on after the rider has begun to pay out.
- Some income riders offer annual increases based on inflation and growth.

For these reasons, income riders have become very popular.

Applying income riders to a retirement plan offers many choices. Since income riders can be used for qualified and non-qualified annuities, they can be arranged to supplement Social Security and pensions, assisting to offset or minimize income tax.

Taxability of Deferred Annuity Distributions

Last in, first out (LIFO) is a term related to the distribution of funds from an annuity contract. The principal or premiums of an annuity fund the contract. Once funded, the contract earns interest. The interest is the "last" of the funds to enter the contract.

When a withdrawal is made, the interest is distributed "first" (last in, first out) and is 100 percent taxable. Once all the tax-deferred interest is distributed, the principal will be distributed. At that time, if the funds are non-qualified, then the only taxable portion of the annuity is the interest earned. If the annuity is qualified, then all distributions are taxable.

Protecting a Non-qualified Annuity

Non-qualified annuities can be placed in a trust with its own tax identification number. By creating a separate entity, the funds can be protected from being used for long-term care purposes.

Laddering incomes has become popular. By utilizing the income rider for life, many people have established several annuities and arrange them to receive multiple incomes throughout the month. By establishing several annuities, income can be taken from one annuity while the others continue to grow. Others may be utilized at a later date, creating a stronger total income and offsetting inflation. There are income riders built to manage inflation. The most beneficial attribute an income rider contributes to a retirement portfolio is the element that the income is for life, regardless of whether the annuity runs out of money. Some income riders have inflation features that continue to keep pace with inflation, even if the annuity runs out of money. If the recipient of the income passes away with money remaining in the annuity, then it passes down to the beneficiary, sometimes tax free.

For More Information

For more in-depth information, please reference article 5, "Considering Fixed Index Annuities."

CHAPTER 11 REVIEW QUESTIONS

1. Fixed index annuities offer downside protection, eliminating the risk of loss with conservative growth potential.

   TRUE   FALSE

2. Funds placed in fixed index annuities are not invested in the market. Funds are placed with the insurance company and invested in the insurance company's portfolio. The insurance company sees fit as to how the fixed index funds are invested.

   TRUE   FALSE

3. Bonuses, caps, spreads, and participation rates work in coordination with the results of the crediting method generated and are used with

   A. Immediate annuities.
   B. Fixed annuities.
   C. Fixed indexed annuities.

4. Annuities are the only financial vehicle other than Social Security and a pension that can provide an income stream for life.

   TRUE   FALSE

5. Income riders have become very popular and have many advantages when creating an income stream for life without annuitizing.

TRUE   FALSE

6. Once an income rider is activated, even though it may run out of money, it will continue to pay out for the life of the insured, regardless.

TRUE   FALSE

7. When an annuity is annuitized, it is considered an income rather than an asset.

TRUE   FALSE

Answers: 1. TRUE, 2. TRUE, 3. C, 4. TRUE, 5. TRUE, 6. TRUE, 7. TRUE

CHAPTER 12

Balancing Qualified Funds with Permanent Life Insurance

Besides annuities, the other type of non-qualified plan is permanent life insurance, which has cash value. Permanent life insurance is structured to last a lifetime. A permanent life insurance contract that is designed to provide cash value during retirement is the only retirement tool that utilizes the first in, first out (FIFO) distribution method providing tax-free principal withdrawals that offset the taxability of qualified funds and provide a tax-free death benefit.

There are two types of permanent life insurance: whole life and universal life. Traditional whole life insurance provides strong guarantees with few uncertainties and is known to be a comprehensive program for retirement planning. Universal life insurance can be built to resemble a whole life program, but it is somewhat of an in-between plan because it can be structured to resemble a whole life plan and a term plan. Like term insurance, a universal life plan can be built to provide insurance for a limited time by adjusting the amount of the premium. In order to extend the policy beyond the set period, the insured individual would increase the premium and extend the length of coverage.

Some policies have evolved to mirror the growth mechanisms found in certain annuities, allowing opportunities for greater growth. Providing minimum guarantees on growth gives the policy owner an opportunity to help grow his or her cash value.

Most permanent life policies have surrender charge periods. Although surrender periods can be avoided at a cost, they should be considered when designing a policy. The length of the surrender charge can affect a death benefit and impact the cash value positively or negatively. Eliminating or shortening a surrender charge period either reduces the face value or takes away from cash value accumulation. It can take several years for the cash value to accumulate, unless you deposit a large single premium. Permanent life insurance should be looked at as a place to house funds to be used in the distant future, not immediately.

When using a life insurance policy for retirement planning, it is important to be aware of how a modified endowment contract (MEC, pronounced "meck") can affect your options. A MEC is a life insurance policy that has been funded with more money than US tax laws allow. Single premium (one large amount of money) funding of a life insurance policy may create a MEC if the policy is funded to a paid-up status within the completion of seven years. By the government setting limits, individuals are prevented from overfunding a life insurance contract, which would create greater tax-free deferred growth. Also, these limits prevent tax-free opportunities that would otherwise be borrowed from taxable funds. After the seventh year, the policy must not exceed the premium guideline, which would also create the policy to become a MEC. Without the premium guideline, an individual could overfund the policy in the eighth year or later.

By not funding the policy to a MEC, the principal funds are distributed before interest without taxability while a person is alive. This is the primary purpose for using a life insurance policy for accumulating retirement funds. Interest is taxable once the principal premiums are completely distributed, which can be several years later.

A MEC reverses this method, causing the interest to be distributed before the principal and causing a taxable event upon the first distribution. Life insurance policies designed for retirement should never be funded to reach the MEC. Once a policy becomes a MEC, it is irreversible. Some life insurance policies are designed to adjust so that a MEC won't occur by automatically increasing the death benefit or by returning the excess premium. A MEC is something to be aware of but not overly concerned about since insurance companies have created systems to work within the rules protecting your contract from becoming a MEC or informing you.

Why Permanent Life Insurance?

There are five reasons why permanent life insurance works well when planning for retirement. It:

- accumulates cash for supplemental income;
- allows for cash withdrawals for incidental purchases during the accumulation phases and in retirement;
- assists with estate tax if needed;
- provides your spouse or family with a tax-free death benefit;
- offers unique tax advantages used to balance and offset qualified income during retirement.

Cash Accumulation for Supplemental Income for Retirement

A life insurance policy that is structured for retirement income will do the following:

- Accumulate cash to supplement qualified income for tax purposes and incidental purchases. Cash value in a life insurance policy is non-qualified; therefore, the only value that is taxable is interest earned. Life insurance follows a favorable tax distribution method of first in, first out (FIFO), as described above.
- Accumulate cash for a down market in order to support everyday income because life insurance has guarantees on cash-value growth. By using this source of cash for income, the principal and potential earning of the investment portfolio will have time to regenerate. Life insurance cash value will regenerate once the investment portfolio has recuperated and the income need is switched back to the investment portfolio.
- Pay out a lump sum or an annuitization, tax free, in the event of death. In turn, the funds can be used to support a spouse as income, compensate for negative investments, and provide security for the estate's assets against estate tax.

Distribution Options before and during Retirement

Whole life and universal life insurance can be structured to provide cash value during the accumulation phase and in retirement. As additional premium enters a life insurance policy, cash value and the death benefit increase, based on the type and terms of the contract.

There are two ways of taking money out of a life insurance policy without lapsing the policy: a direct withdrawal or a loan. Both methods will have an impact on the policy. When designing a policy, it is important to understand and manage its effects. Discussing these options prior to choosing and designing a policy is imperative.

Direct Withdrawal Method for Distribution

When funds are removed using a withdrawal, the cash and death values (face value plus cash value) will decrease. Structuring the policy appropriately, using options from within the plan while also coordinating death and cash values, is important in order to maintain the original death benefit.

For example, using a universal life policy, John purchased a policy with a $500,000 face value to accumulate funds for retirement. As he adds extra premium to the policy, the cash value and the death benefit increase. Over thirty years, John accumulates $200,000 in cash value above the scheduled premium, increasing the death benefit proportionately. John plans to use the withdrawal method because his intentions were to have a $500,000 death benefit and understands, if he withdraws more than his contribution above the scheduled premium, the death value will drop below the original $500,000. If he dies prematurely, the cash value from the death benefit goes to his beneficiary/beneficiaries directly since he was approved using Option B, or II, "return of account value." Return of account value adds the cash value to the face value to determine a death benefit and is an added cost to the policy. Option A, or I, does not do this. Assume that John takes all elements into consideration in order to meet his expectations. There is no expense to the policy to use the direct withdrawal method.

Loan Methods for Distribution

If John's policy allows him to take funds out as a loan, he can take either a wash loan or a participating loan, based on the terms of the policy.

Figure 12.1: Effect of a Wash Loan

	Policy	Loan
Cash value	$200,000	
Loan		$20,000
Adjusted cash value	$180,000	
8% Growth	+$14,400	
5% Loan interest charge		-$1,000
5% Interest growth applied to loan		+$1,000
Policy growth	$14,400	$0

The wash loan separates the loan from the cash value while maintaining the death benefit. It charges the policy a predetermined fixed rate for the loan. At the same time, it credits the policy the same fixed rate, creating a wash. The cash value continues to grow, based on the reduced cash value.

If John's policy offers a participating loan, the face value remains the same because the loan stays in the cash value. The interest charge created by the loan decreases the cash value. However, the loaned amount continues to grow within the cash value. If the cash value grows 8 percent and the interest rate on the loan is 5 percent, the loaned funds generate 3 percent more than they pay out in interest ($20,000 x .08 growth = $1,600; interest charge is $1,000; difference between the two is $600, or 3 percent of $20,000).

Figure 12.2: Effect of a Participating Loan

Cash value	$200,000
Growth of 8%	$16,000
Loan interest at 5%	-$1,000
Policy growth	$15,000

The difference between the growth and the loan interest is 3 percent, as displayed. Since the loan value is not subtracted from the cash value, the cash value and loan amount continue to grow together at the 8 percent rate, 3 percent higher than the loan rate. In Figure 12.2, if the interest rate on the loan is 5 percent and the policy has no growth, the cash value will experience a loss. Generally, loan options are detailed in the contract.

Cash Accumulation and Distribution for Unexpected Purchases

Both whole life and universal life insurance can be structured to provide cash value during the accumulation phase, as well as in retirement. For example, Mary is forty-five years old, is married, and has three children. She has been contributing to her permanent life insurance policy for the past fifteen years. She and four of her friends decide to tour Europe for three weeks. The cost of the vacation is $10,000. Mary does not want to use family funds so she withdraws $10,000 from her life insurance policy. Based on the options provided in the contract, she can take or borrow the funds and reimburse the policy or allow the policy to regenerate.

The Role of Term Life Insurance and Your Retirement Portfolio

Term insurance, although very popular, is not entirely helpful when planning for retirement income because there is no cash value. Term insurance is built to accommodate unexpected death during the accumulation phase, providing resources to satisfy debts and short-term investment failures for the family. It is also used for business partnership agreements and support for business debt in the event that a key person or business partner unexpectedly dies. Term insurance can be incorporated into a retirement plan but will unlikely be a considerable asset during retirement unless death occurs within the period of coverage or is converted into a permanent policy. Sometimes it is beneficial to consider converting a term policy into a permanent policy. A term policy conversion is the process of exchanging the policy for a permanent one. A term policy conversion may take place only within the conversion period.

Group term policies do not convert to permanent plans. Generally, when a person leaves an employer, the former employee may have the option to convert the group policy into a private term policy, but not further.

Health underwriting is unnecessary when converting an individual term policy to a permanent policy. The new policy is based on your age at the time of conversion. For example, a woman buys a thirty-year term policy at twenty-five years old. In the fifteenth year (at age forty), she is diagnosed with diabetes (insurable risk factor). She decides she would like protection for a longer period of time and converts her policy into a permanent plan with coverage to 120 years old. Although a new health exam is not required, her new premiums are based on the calculations at age forty.

Protecting a Life Insurance Policy

Permanent insurance policies are often held in irrevocable trusts that are designed to function according to the individual's needs while protecting the policy from Medicaid consideration. The look-back period (waiting period) is shorter or non-existent when a policy is placed in the trust as soon as it is issued than if it is placed in the trust after the issue date. In order for this to happen, the trust must be named as the policy owner. Once the look-back period is satisfied, the trust is considered to be outside of the estate.

Should I Have Separate Policies for Each Function?

Although it is not necessary, most individuals choose to separate their policies—using the cash value of one for income purposes and dedicating another to offsetting estate tax. The decision is made based on individual and estate needs.

Combining Annuities and Life Insurance

When combining annuities and permanent life insurance, the advantages are remarkable! Several years ago, I was approached by a husband and wife who were assembling their estate plan. They were advised to take out a $1,000,000 life insurance policy to satisfy potential estate tax upon their deaths. The couple had the choice of a second-to-die plan (a policy with two people insured as one; the policy pays the claim upon the death of the second individual) or an individual plan to be placed on one of the individuals. They chose to place a $1,000,000 policy on the husband. The premium was $24,000 annually. Ten years and $240,000 later, the husband passed away, and an insurance claim was placed. The widow received a check for $1,000,000 tax free. The $1,000,000 was placed in a fixed index annuity with a 10 percent bonus (upfront interest), adding $100,000 to the $1,000,000 and creating an immediate value of $1,100,000. From then on, the contract grew an average of 5 percent annually. Within four years, the annuity had recouped the $240,000 that had been spent as a premium. The policy continued to grow, and when the wife passed away, the family had a substantial value that was applied to estate tax.

If the couple had chosen a second-to-die policy, then the $1,000,000 would not have been released as a claim until the wife passed away. The finances would not have gone into an annuity, and there would not have been a $100,000 bonus to earn interest each year.

For More Information

Please reference article 6, "The Role of Life Insurance and Your Retirement Plan," for more detailed information.

CHAPTER 12 REVIEW QUESTIONS

1. Term insurance has very little use when organizing a retirement plan.

   TRUE   FALSE

2. Permanent life insurance can be designed to accumulate cash value to help offset the impact qualified money can have on taxes.

   TRUE   FALSE

3. Whole life and universal life are permanent policies that will provide the following:

   A. Accumulation for retirement income and estate tax.
   B. Incidental needs during the accumulation phase.
   C. Death benefit, providing the family with financial support.
   D. All of the above.

4. Universal life insurance is considered an in-between program because it:

   A. Can function to resemble a term or a whole life plan.
   B. Came out after whole life and before term.
   C. Offers the flexibility of term insurance.
   D. None of the above.

5. Permanent life insurance policies are often held in irrevocable trusts. After the look-back period, the policy is outside the estate and is not considered when applying to Medicaid.

   TRUE   FALSE

6. By naming the life insurance policy to the trust when the policy is issued by the insurance company, the look-back period is shorter.

   TRUE   FALSE

Answers: 1. TRUE, 2. TRUE, 3. D, 4. A, 5. TRUE, 6. TRUE

Practical Application IV
Identifying and Evaluating Your Annuities and Life Insurance

Now that you have read section 4, let's put things in perspective for you and your own situation. Once the information is gathered, document the information on the worksheets found on the website **www. Positioning4 Retirement.com**. There are worksheets for each category of life insurance and annuities that have been annuitized.

Note: You should have listed your funds that have not been annuitized when you organized your qualified or non-qualified assets in Practical Applications 1, 2, and 3. If you haven't, please go back and list them. This section is for funds that have been annuitized.

Income from an income rider or systematic withdrawals of an annuity is not considered annuitized. However, income received from income riders and systematic withdrawals should be listed here, even though they are not annuitized. The annuity that the income rider is coming from is considered an asset, and the value of the annuity should also be listed under its respective qualified and non-qualified funds. Simply put, the income being received from the income rider goes on this section while the accumulated value of the annuity is an asset and listed in the asset sections.

1. **If you have an immediate annuity, what is it paying out and for how long?**

    Complete the following worksheet:

    WS 5   Non-qualified Income from Immediate Annuities

    Move the value from the worksheet to the spreadsheet.

2. **For annuities that have been annuitized, what is each annuity paying, its frequency, and the date the payout will stop?**

    Complete the following worksheets:

    WS 3   Qualified Income from Annuitized Annuities
    WS 6   Non-qualified Income from Annuitized Annuities

    Move the value from the worksheet to the spreadsheet.

3. **List income(s) coming from income riders and systematic withdrawals.**

   Complete the following worksheets:

   > WS 4   Qualified Incomes from Annuities with Income
   > Riders and Systematic Withdrawals
   > WS 7   Non-qualified Incomes from Annuities with Income
   > Riders and Systematic Withdrawals

   Move the information to the spreadsheet.

4. **If you have life insurance, what type is it—term, universal, or whole life?**

   Complete the following worksheet:

   > WS 21   Life Insurance Policies

   Move the information to the spreadsheet.

5. **Do you have disability insurance?**

   Complete the following worksheet:

   > WS 22   Disability Insurance Policies

   Move the information to the spreadsheet.

   If at anytime assistance is needed, contact the Retirement Education Resource Center of North America, Inc. at 781-763-RERC (7372) or email us at help@ positioning4retirement.com.

SUGGESTIONS, SOLUTIONS, AND OPINIONS

CHAPTER 13

Protect Qualified Assets with an Irrevocable Trust

An irrevocable trust is used to protect assets, minimize estate tax liability, avoid probate, and maintain privacy. They are designed to protect qualified and non-qualified funds. The terms in a qualified retirement trust are written to meet IRS acceptance.

Irrevocable trusts have their own name and identification number that create a taxable entity separate from the donor (also called grantor or settlor). An irrevocable trust, regardless of whether it is funded with qualified or non-qualified funds, will not allow the donor to change the substantive (essential) terms of the trust. The administrative terms, such as the trustee(s) and the state that is interpreting the trust, can be changed by the donor at any time and as often as needed.

One reason for establishing an irrevocable trust is to protect funds from paying long-term care expenses. Medicare (not Medicaid) pays for approximately the first one hundred days of care in a treatment facility, provided progress is made. After one hundred days, a person must pay for treatment from personal assets or from a long-term-care insurance policy. Planning ahead permits most assets to be protected in an irrevocable trust, creating an opportunity to utilize public programs, such as Medicaid. The only assets that cannot be protected in a trust are qualified assets that were accumulated by the living donor.

Funds placed in an irrevocable trust must satisfy the look-back period in order to be considered outside the estate. Once outside the estate, the asset is not considered by Medicaid. The look-back period is not grandfathered and begins the day the Medicaid application is filed. Currently, the look-back period is five years and can change at any time due to decisions made in Congress and each state.

For qualified funds, the trust is designed as an irrevocable IRS retirement plan trust. Similar to all irrevocable trusts, it is designed to address second marriages, spendthrift spouses, and advancing generational wealth. The IRS Retirement Plan trust specifically follows the IRS regulations governing plan distribution. While alive, the donor must receive RMDs as usual with qualified funds. Once the donor is deceased, the trust is then funded with the donor's qualified funds, and the trustee is put in charge. At that time, funds are considered outside the beneficiary's estate for tax purposes.

IRA owners can name trusts as beneficiaries as a way to better control post-death distributions and restrict access for beneficiaries who might otherwise squander large inherited IRAs. The trust as beneficiary insures that the IRA funds are protected from creditors and bankruptcy since the trust assets are not actually owned by your surviving spouse.

You want to leave your spouse the annual IRA income, but after his or her death, you want to make sure the IRA goes to your children and grandchildren who are generally taxed at a lower rate. Therefore, you bring another party into the equation, the trustee, to act on behalf of the beneficiary. The trustee should be a trusted family member or advisor that will make sound business decisions on behalf of the beneficiary.

If there are multiple beneficiaries, they must all use the life expectancy of the beneficiary who is oldest. (If you have three children close in age, it does not have much impact on their respective required minimum distribution periods, which are the beneficiaries' stretch periods. However, if the beneficiaries have large differences in age, you should use a trust for each.)

Obviously, there will always be income tax deferral benefits with naming a surviving spouse individually as the designated beneficiary of the IRA, although these benefits are significantly diminished once the IRA owner and his or her spouse are both over the age 70½. For many people, there are worse outcomes than not being able to obtain maximum income tax deferral for IRA assets.

Additional Legal Documents for Consideration

Other than assets in the retirement trust, an attorney may recommend trust and legal strategies based on family dynamics, assets, and objectives. These documents create a comprehensive legal plan with the objective to:

- give someone you trust the ability to manage your estate and fulfill your wishes when you are unable to;
- minimize your need to pay for long-term care in a facility by using government programs, such as PACE, veteran programs, and Medicaid;
- minimize or eliminate your exposure to state and federal estate tax;
- protect disabled family members;
- maintain privacy and avoid probate when you pass away.

Power of Attorney

This document gives your fiduciary (called the attorney-in-fact) the authority to handle a broad range of financial transactions on your behalf. The fiduciary can be a family member, friend, or third party, such as an attorney. It is important that the fiduciary is someone you trust emphatically since he or she has power over your financial well-being. The power of attorney is durable; that is, it continues to be legally effective in the event of a disability.

Living Will

This is a declaration and acts as a foundation for doctors and health-care agents to know your personal wishes when your health is diminishing. It declares whether you wish to have life-saving measures, such as being put on a breathing device, or wish to have an uninterrupted death.

Revocable Trust

Assets and funds that are used for everyday activities, such as checking, savings, and investment accounts, are placed and held in this trust. The revocable trust is designed to avoid the expense and delay of probate while maintaining privacy when you die. While alive, assets can be moved in and out of the trust. Upon death, the trust becomes irrevocable, and the trustee must follow the direction that was established by you in the trust. Generally, the donor or donors are the trustee or trustees. If married, both partners are named as donors and trustees. An appointed successor trustee is named in the document, whether single or married, to fulfill your wishes in the event that none of the prior trustees is capable. This type of trust is fully amendable during your lifetime. Any changes in circumstances can be dealt with in an amendment to the trust.

Will with a Pour-over Provision

This document works in coordination with a revocable trust. It is a will that presents your wishes when you die. However, this will has a pour-over provision, which pours the probatable assets into the revocable trust. For example, a married couple flies to Florida and purchases property. The husband and wife do not put it in a trust. On their way home, they are in an accident, and both die. Since it is not in a trust, the property needs to be probated, which follows the direction of their will. If your will has a pour-over provision, any assets that are not in a trust are directed to follow the provision and go through probate to the revocable trust. The disclosure of the asset is public; however, the distribution of the assets remains private.

Real Estate Trusts

Real estate trusts are used to avoid probate, reduce estate tax liability, and provide Medicaid protection. In general, a real estate trust is a separate entity with its own tax identification number. Placing property in the real estate trust removes it from your estate, which will minimize or help avoid paying federal and/or state estate tax when you pass away. A real estate trust may also help you qualify for Medicaid benefits if you need long-term care in a skilled nursing facility. It dictates your wishes to the trustee for the property upon your demise. There are many types of real estate trusts, and your attorney will take each type into consideration to determine which will best fit your situation.

Special Needs Trusts

A special needs trust is an irrevocable trust designed to protect a family member that is disabled and collecting state and/or federal benefits. In the event that you pass away and leave money to the special needs person collecting state or federal benefits, the individual's benefit is halted until he or she has used the inherited asset. The language in a special needs trust allows the individual collecting benefits to receive income without affecting his or her benefit. The trustee should not distribute more than the allowable limit.

There are many other documents for all types of situations and reasons. Wording the proper language and designing the particulars of the trust are important. Coordinating and protecting assets for your family while limiting legal and tax liabilities are the ultimate objectives in most plans. An attorney that is knowledgeable in estate and Medicaid planning should lead the discussions to creating a successful trust.

For More Information

For more details, reference article 7, "Understanding the Irrevocable IRS Qualified Retirement Trust," in the article section.

CHAPTER 13 REVIEW QUESTIONS

1. 1. The word "irrevocable" in relation to a trust means "you may not change the substantive terms of the trust."

    TRUE   FALSE

2. While alive, the donor of an irrevocable trust can change:

    A. Whatever he or she wants.
    B. Only the trustee(s) and state of interpretation.
    C. Beneficiaries and trustee(s).
    D. Nothing.

3. Once qualified assets are placed in an irrevocable trust, the person placing them in the trust cannot use the principal without violating the terms of the trust.

    TRUE   FALSE

4. An irrevocable retirement trust will remove the asset from the estate:

    A. Immediately after the death of the donor.
    B. Provided the look-back period is complete.
    C. Five years after the death of the donor, provided the look-back period doesn't change.
    D. Three months after the document is recorded with the state.

5. One purpose when using an irrevocable retirement trust is to:

    A. Protect assets for future generations.
    B. Avoid paying RMDs while alive and afterward.
    C. Continue deferring tax after 70½ years old.
    D. All of the above.

Answers: 1. TRUE, 2. B, 3. TRUE, 4. A, 5. A

CHAPTER 14

Providing Resources and Protection with Long-term Care Insurance (LTCI)

People spend time and energy worrying about whether they will have enough money to retire. They watch their funds grow one day and shrivel the next day. They pay so much attention to how much they have and very little or no attention to protecting it.

A long-term care insurance policy, if properly designed, will provide your family with financial, physical, and emotional resources while protecting your assets. Financially, it is a way to self-insure, using assets to pay for coverage, entirely or while getting through the look-back period. Hopefully trusts have been established well in advance so the look-back period is not an issue. Since look-back periods can change and are not grandfathered, a long-term care insurance policy can create reassurance and, most important, provide the family with resources and support.

A long-term care insurance policy is a disability plan. It doesn't replace incomes as a typical disability plan would; instead, it provides income to pay for necessary services in the event of accident, illness, or aging and being unable to do everyday tasks. Once the insured is unable to perform two of the six activities of daily living (bathing, continence, dressing, eating, toileting, and transferring), referred to as ADLs, the insurance company will reimburse expenses needed to compensate for these activities. A long-term care policy will provide income for your family to pay for:

- **Home health aides,** which provide bathing, cooking, and feeding.
- **Homemaking services**, which provide for cleaning, doing laundry, and shopping.
- **Respite care and adult day care,** which allows the caregiver to get rest. A common concern is the health and well-being of the primary caregiver, usually the spouse.
- **Assisted living** and **skilled nursing** facilities.
- **Hospice** care if needed.

A long-term care insurance policy can provide services without cost to assist the family in need. A care coordinator is available either by phone or in person (based on the contract) to support family members in the care process. With experience and knowledge, a care coordinator has all the resources to find and hire help for services and equipment.

When families learn that their loved one needs extended care, oftentimes their reaction depends on whether or not they have a long-term care insurance policy. If they have a long-term care policy, then they are concerned; they are looking for direction and help to implement a claim while caring and setting up a plan for their loved one.

If they don't have a policy, there is:

- **Fear** of the unknown—what is expected of them, what is going to happen next, and how will it be handled.
- **Despair** in knowing they are obligated to do something they may not be prepared to do or want to do.
- **Panic** with how their new responsibility is going to cut into their life, how it will affect their job or career, or how it will take time away from their family (especially if they have children at home).
- **Anxiety** concerning what to do first and whom to turn to for help.
- **An overwhelming feeling** of a sudden unexpected and often unwanted responsibility.

The problems that not having a long-term care insurance policy presents can have lasting results. They can separate a family if the majority of the work and responsibility is put on one member. They can place undue pressure on the spouse, and the spouse-caretaker can become in need as well. The individual needing care would rather die than watch his or her family and finances struggle.

Often, the family thinks that an LTCI policy will take the responsibility of caring for relatives away from them; however, this is not true. An LTCI policy will not remove the family's responsibility to care for their loved one; it provides physical, emotional, and financial resources to pay for help. It allows the family to be in control and supervise the administration of care. The family may also participate in the care as desired. LTCI protects the family's income and assets by providing income to pay for the necessary services, relieving the threat of spending down assets.

In a situation where there is no family, the individual would put his or her expectations in the hands of a third-party advocate to oversee the administration of the policy. This can be a friend, a church member, a fiduciary (i.e., an attorney, a senior advisor, or a professional caregiver) who will work with the care coordinator appointed by the insurance company.

Like all insurance, health and age play a role in securing long-term care insurance. Therefore, it is important to obtain a long-term care policy when you are healthy, the younger the better. The underwriting process is necessary to determine if the applicant is eligible to be insured. Underwriting a long-term care application is unique because the insurance company evaluates the risk and the negative disabling effect on the activities of daily living (not necessarily death).

Many people who have had cancer feel that history prevents them from obtaining long-term care insurance, but this is not true. Several insurance companies will insure cancer victims because cancer may have predictability factors. Uncontrolled high blood pressure is an equal risk for insurability since it may lead to a stroke or heart attack with less predictability, potentially affecting the activities of daily living for a longer period of time. Insurance companies vary in whom they will insure, but it is not impossible to become insured if you have a serious illness, although it is less likely.

The Employee Benefit Research Institute reported in June 2012, "Among nursing home entrants, purchase of long-term care insurance (LTCI) has also increased steadily during the past decade, but coverage remains low (14 percent in 2010)." This means that 86 percent of the individuals that entered a nursing home were self-insuring by spending down their assets, winging it, or using Medicaid. By self-insuring with the use of a long-term care insurance policy, qualified funds are protected from Medicaid unless the policy runs out of money. The assets would need to be spent down to state limits in order to receive Medicaid benefits. It is important to have a policy adequate enough to fit your potential needs. Your policy should take you beyond the look-back period and to the end of your life.

Nursing-home rates on a national level are increasing at a rate of 4.1 percent annually. One of three issues that long-term care insurance companies are confronted with is maintaining inflation. A typical long-term care policy will offer cost-of-living adjustment (COLA) vehicles that adjust for inflation. With the markets being difficult to predict over the last decade, insurance companies have had to rethink their positions, and several companies have even left the long-term care insurance market.

Insurance companies have also had to address low policy-lapse rates and the fact that policyholders are outliving their policies. Families are supporting policy premiums, understanding the consequences that the policy addresses. Insurance companies depend on policies lapsing when developing the policy because this leads to a premium and profitability. The lapse rate on long-term care policies is low. In many states like Massachusetts, it is mandated by law that a family member be notified in the event that the premium of a long-term care policy is not paid on time, allowing the family member to satisfy the premium. Knowing the value that the policy presents to the family and the individual's estate, policyholders (and/or their families) are not letting policies lapse as frequently.

The market for long-term insurance is approximately forty-five years old. Insurance companies are beginning to see the effect that LTC is having on the industry and are coming to the realization that individuals are outliving the policy value and the benefit period, therefore exhausting the policy. Over the last few years, they have had to reconsider the market and their position in it. The companies remaining are adjusting their programs and becoming gender sensitive, adjusting the number of qualifying ADLs, inflation mechanisms, benefit periods, premiums, and services.

Tax Incentive for Qualified Long-term Care Policy Holders

Individuals that hold a tax-qualified long-term care policy have a potential tax deduction. A tax-qualified plan must meet the standards established in the Health Insurance Portability and Accountability Act of 1996 (HIPAA). The deduction is based on the age of the individual at the end of the tax year, the insurance premium, and the individual's adjusted gross income (AGI). The deductible portion of the insurance premium is the excess of 10 percent of the person's AGI prior to age sixty-five or 7.5 percent for those sixty-five and older. This excess is treated as a medical expense. The 2014 deductions are as follows:

Age	2014
39 or younger	$370
40–49	$700
50–59	$1,400
60–69	$3,720
70 and older	$4,660

(IRS Bulletin 2013-47)

The deduction is most useful when the individual has medical expenses beyond those being reimbursed by the LTCI policy.

For those that are self-employed, the incentive is different. The premium of a long-term care insurance policy is treated as health insurance and is taken off the top and included in the AGI calculation.

There are states that offer tax incentives as well, some equal to the federal guidelines. To determine the incentive that your state offers, search www.partnershipforlongtermcare.com/statetaxincentives.html.

Outliving Your Policy

If you live beyond the scope of the policy and the proper legal documents were put in place to allow them to reach beyond the look-back period, Medicaid will step in. If the proper documents are not in place and you are not beyond the look-back period, assets will need to be spent down until they meet the levels set by the state you live in. This is why it is important to have a well-coordinated plan utilizing private and public programs assembled with the help of your team of professionals.

Case Study 14.1

LTCI supports the family with resources, tools, and outside help. Many adult children promise never to put their parents in a nursing home and will be there for them when the time comes. That is exactly what my brothers and I told our parents. So far, we have been able to hold that promise. Unless anything happens to me, my brothers, my wife, and my children, nieces and nephews, we should be able to keep our promise.

In her eighties, my mother is able to function independently. My father passed away in 2008 from cancer at eighty-three years old. He was independent, strong-willed, and private. When my father was diagnosed with cancer, I had little knowledge about his financial situation. Upon the diagnosis, my father revealed his finances. He had money in his 401(k), money in bank CDs, and a home that was paid off. But he lacked a long-term care policy and an estate plan.

My mother's financial welfare would have been jeopardized in this situation since her assets weren't protected. Her husband was the primary breadwinner and had a substantial portion of his wealth in qualified assets. If placed in a skilled nursing facility, his qualified assets would have been spent down to the point where my mother would have been in financial disaster. In her late seventies at the time, she needed assistance to care for her husband. Trips to the doctor's office became an issue because my father had done all the driving while he was well. He was unable to bathe himself, maintain the home, or shop. My mother was forced to take over for the entirety of his illness, which lasted for eighteen months. Help came in to the house for three hours a week for personal care and three hours a week for home care (all paid by Elder Care/Medicare). Someone came to help my father bathe twice a week; he was more comfortable with a trained stranger than a family member.

Our biggest concern was that my mother was going to transition from caregiver to the one needing care. We had very few choices; my father believed in insurance but didn't know much about long-term care insurance. Like many others, he did not see the purpose. We quickly began to understand the value of long-term care insurance; it not only helps preserve the financial landscape for a surviving spouse but also provides resources. A long-term care insurance policy would have satisfied many of the issues that we were confronted with.

Case Study 14.2

This is a very common story. A family has a back-up system five or six people deep including siblings, relatives, and friends. One parent is rushed to the hospital and then transferred to a rehabilitation facility. The facility determines that the patient cannot go home without extensive twenty-four-hour professional help, equipped with medical supplies necessary to keep the parent alive. The family is able to care for the parent until the situation becomes so bad that it is impossible to keep the parent out of the nursing home.

Through no fault of their own, the family learns what it means to spend down assets at a rate of $12,000 a month until their parent is able to qualify for Medicaid. Several agonizing years after Medicare pays its one hundred days, the individual dies and was never able to qualify for Medicaid. It costs the family $408,000 out of pocket. A long-term care policy would have satisfied this expense and relieved the family of financial burden.

Case Study 14.3

One day I received a phone call from a man whose father had lived independently but became sick and was placed in a rehabilitation facility. As the one-hundredth day approached, the patient and his family were concerned about his future ability to care for himself. The father was no longer independent and could not go home without round-the-clock supervision; he needed to be placed in a nursing home.

I offered to help and met with his father who divulged that his house had been paid off and wanted to pass it on to his family. Unfortunately, he did not have LTCI, and he never protected the property from the threat of a Medicaid lien. After his death, the house was sold, and the Medicaid lien was satisfied. The stress, aggravation, disappointment, and uprooting affected the whole family. The father thought that, since the house was paid for, it was his and no one could take it away.

Case Study 14.4

On the brighter side, another client had the insight to purchase a long-term care policy. She was a nurse in an Alzheimer's unit and watched families scramble to pay for services until Medicaid stepped in. Eventually, she was admitted into the same Alzheimer's unit that she had supervised. She had purchased a long-term care policy because she had not wanted her family to experience what she had witnessed. Because she was prepared, she was able to protect 90 percent of her assets for her family.

All these stories took place within four years of one another. Based on information provided by the Employee Benefit Research Institute dated June 2012, in 2010, 86 percent of nursing home entrants over the age of sixty-five did not have long-term care insurance. They also note that "those who reported being most likely to enter a nursing home in the near future were also less likely to purchase LTCI."

For More Information

Refer to article 8, "The Role of Long-term Care Insurance and Your Retirement Plan," at the end of this book.

CHAPTER 14 REVIEW QUESTIONS

1. A long-term care insurance policy provides resources and assistance to reach out to services that are needed to assist the caregiver and family physically, emotionally, and financially.

   TRUE   FALSE

2. What percentage of people entering nursing homes in 2010 were either self-insuring, winging it, or on Medicaid?

   A. 10%
   B. 14%
   C. 50%
   D. 86%

3. The use of a long-term care insurance policy can assist the individual to reach beyond the look-back period.

   TRUE   FALSE

4. Over the past few years, companies offering long-term care insurance have changed the design and structure of their policies because:

   A. People are outliving their policies.
   B. Policyholders and their families are not allowing the policy to lapse due to the nature of the policy and are supporting the premium.
   C. Nursing home costs are increasing at a national rate of 4.1 percent annually, and inflation compounders are a concern due to difficult markets.
   D. All of the above.

5. A long-term care insurance policy will eliminate all responsibilities for the family, allowing the individual to control his or her destiny with dignity.

   TRUE   FALSE

6. If an individual were to die at home, then the individual would not need any of the long-term care concerns mentioned.

   TRUE   FALSE

Answers: 1. TRUE, 2. D, 3. TRUE, 4. D, 5. FALSE, 6. TRUE,

CHAPTER 15

Protecting Qualified and Real Assets by Self-insuring

Protecting assets by self-insuring means that assets will be spent down to pay for long-term care (LTC) needs, which includes home health care, assisted living, or skilled extended care. Medicare will contribute up to one hundred days in a facility after three days in a hospital. After that, the cost of the individual's care is paid through the spending down of the family's assets to the allowable limit until Medicaid contributes.

As covered in the previous chapter, an alternative way of self-insuring is to use assets to support an adequate long-term care insurance (LTCI) policy. Using this method ensures that the estate will not be depleted.

Self-insuring can be structured in several ways, and each of these methods avoids the use of Medicaid. Based on a financial analysis prepared by a CPA, programs can be established based on your financial ability.

Health is a determining factor when structuring a financial plan. If the individual's health is concluded to be uninsurable, self-insuring with the utilization of a long-term care policy is not an option. Annuities may offer elements, such as extended-care riders, which increase the lifetime payout without proof of insurability.

If the individual is insurable, then he or she has multiple options. If the individual feels that funding a long-term care policy is beneficial, then there are several methods of funding.

- The individual can pay the premium of the long-term care policy from investments or cash on hand.
- The individual can institute an annuity established with guarantees that earns interest to pay the premium. By placing the annuity in an irrevocable trust that is designed to do this, the principal is protected and never used.
- If the individual's assets are not strong enough to fund either of these options, then he or she may elect to utilize an annuity with an income rider. This method will work down the principal of the funds placed in the annuity; however, once a long-term care claim is placed and the elimination period is satisfied, the annuity funding the LTC policy will continue to grow and can be reinvested. Based on the annuity contract, the income rider can be turned off, and the annuity will begin to regenerate what it had paid out.
- Long-term care costs can be paid out of investments, and a life insurance policy is established to refund the cost of the insurance policy/policies to the family upon the insured's death.
- The investment funds the premium of a life insurance policy with a long-term care rider, which is backed by the face value of the policy, in part or in full, depending on what is utilized for extended care.

Case Study 15.1

John is sixty years old and healthy. His financial analysis reflects a value of $2,000,000 of retirement assets. John qualifies for a long-term care, standalone policy as well as a life insurance policy with an LTC rider. After careful consideration, John determined that the life insurance with an LTC rider suited his plan. If he had not qualified for a long-term care insurance rider but qualified for a life insurance policy, a living benefit rider would suit him because a living benefit rider does not require LTC underwriting. John is approved for a $1,000,000 life policy with an LTC rider.

He can fund the policy using investments, annuity interest, or income payouts. The vehicles housing the funding methods, as well as the insurance policy, are housed in a trust that is designed specifically to fulfill John's objectives. If John dies never having used the long-term care portion of the policy, then the face value goes to the estate as designated in the trust. If John uses a portion of the long-term care rider, then those expenses reduce the face value, and the remaining face value is released upon death to the trust. Then, the trust distributes the funds according to John's wish.

There are limitations to John's decision, including the following.

- Some policies require premium payments until death, and others offer a waiver of premium after the elimination period is met. John will pay until death.
- There is no cost of living adjustment (COLA) utilized to maintain inflation.
- The long-term care portion can be limited to a percentage of the face value on a monthly payout. Based on a $1,000,000 policy with a 3 percent monthly benefit, the insured will have up to $30,000 a month in reimbursements to apply to extended care expenses.
- Some contracts require the policy to maintain a minimum face value.

A rider attached to a life insurance policy and a living benefit rider have definite differences and should be thoroughly examined by your insurance professional in conjunction with your team of professionals in order to make the decision.

Medicare and Medicaid Working Together

Whether or not you are using insurance programs, it is imperative to research government-funded programs with long-term care policies. Programs such as PACE (Program of All-Inclusive Care for the Elderly), which is Medicare and Medicaid supported, are becoming increasingly popular. PACE provides a daycare program, oftentimes with transportation to and from the facility. However, PACE is not available everywhere. PACE began in California in the 1990s and has slowly migrated across the country touching population-dense areas that will support the program with Medicare and Medicaid benefits. PACE is available to everyone, regardless of financial integrity.

The financial qualifications vary by state. For instance, some states, such as Massachusetts, consider income only. If you exceed the Massachusetts income limits, you are still eligible to participate in the PACE program, but you must contribute to the cost. In other states, such as Rhode Island, financial eligibility and premium are based on income and assets.

Once enrolled in PACE, a person's total care is assigned to a team of professionals—social workers and doctors specializing in all areas of health care. Individuals that do not qualify for Medicaid can use a long-term care policy to offset any outstanding premium.

Veteran Programs

Reach out to your local Veterans Affairs (VA) administrator if you are a veteran or the spouse of a veteran, especially if you are totally disabled and served in active combat. Applying for VA benefits for a veteran is limited to veterans, VA administrators, and government-approved attorneys. Attorneys are prohibited from charging for applying for VA benefits for an individual but will be helpful if the veteran program is part of establishing an estate plan, especially when Medicaid planning is involved. Coordinating veteran and Medicaid benefits is important since qualifying for one can limit or prohibit you from qualifying for the other. The severity of the long-term care need determines the type and extent of care VA will provide.

Summing It Up

Without the utilization of one or a combination of these options, qualified funds are at the mercy of being used to support extended-care plans, such as home health care, assisted living, and skilled nursing facilities.

This is how it works:

- Qualified and non-qualified assets are spent down until they meet the acceptable levels set by the state.
- Once the assets are spent down, real assets such as a home or homes are taken into consideration based on state guidelines.
- Once all assets are exhausted down to the state's allowable levels, Medicaid will step in and assume the responsibility of your care.
- Qualified incomes, such as pensions and Social Security, are signed over to the facility.

For More Information

Refer to article 8, "The Role of Long-term Care Insurance and Your Retirement Plan," at the end of this book.

CHAPTER 15 REVIEW QUESTIONS

1. An individual has the following option(s) to provide financial protection when the need for extended care arises.

   A. Three options—self-insuring, which includes spending down assets in order to qualify for Medicaid; Medicaid if the assets are less than the state allowable limit; and a long-term care insurance plan.
   B. Only two options—Medicaid and Medicare will cover all areas of extended care.
   C. Only Medicare, not Medicaid, covers extended care completely.
   D. A long-term care insurance policy is the only way to protect qualified and real assets.

2. A long-term care insurance policy will eliminate all responsibilities for the family.

   TRUE   FALSE

3. If an individual were to die at home, then the individual would not need any of the long-term care programs mentioned.

   TRUE   FALSE

4. Qualified incomes such as Social Security and pensions are utilized when paying for a skilled nursing facility through Medicaid.

   TRUE   FALSE

Answers: 1. A, 2. FALSE, 3. TRUE, 4. TRUE

CHAPTER 16

Putting It All Together
What Does It Mean?

Positioning retirement assets in conjunction with other assets is imperative to determining the type of retirement lifestyle you wish to live. It is possible to maximize your retirement income, reduce your taxable environment, and protect your family's interest.

Remember in chapter 5 when we analyzed the effect that qualified funds have on Social Security and income tax? While case study 5.1 had minimal to no taxable income because the subject's income was below the threshold, case studies 5.2 and 5.3 were different.

This following graph illustrates case study 5.1. The individual's total income is $38,233, of which $25,733 is qualified income (Social Security, pension, qualified distributions and taxable interest from non-qualified funds) placing the person in the non-taxable category on the Social Security Taxable chart found in chapter 4.

Figure 16.1: Case Study 5.1 (from page 28)

The principal from the non-qualified fund ($12,500) is not considered since it has already been taxed. The adjusted gross income from case study 5.1 is $13,908 and is below the taxable threshold. The individual will pay a minimal ($221) federal income tax. If the person's taxable income was $11,500, there would be no tax due.

The following two graphs come from case study 5.2 in chapter 5. Figure 16.2 illustrates the case as presented, while figure 16.3 shows the effect on taxable income when a Roth account replaces a small portion of the qualified account.

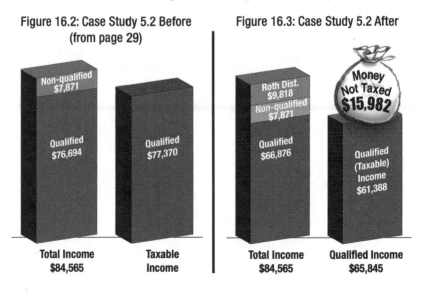

Figure 16.2: Case Study 5.2 Before (from page 29)

Figure 16.3: Case Study 5.2 After

In this case, figure 16.2 presents $76,694 of qualified income plus $7,871 of non-qualified distribution, creating the individual's total income of $84,565. Of that total, 91.5 percent, or $77,370, is taxable, as displayed in case study 5.2, and 8.5 percent, or $7,195, remains not taxable. Of that non-taxed amount, 85.7 percent, or $6,164 comes from the non-qualified income principal, and 14.3 percent, or $1,031, is the individual's Social Security benefit that is not taxed.

Now let's examine the effect of positioning assets, replacing $9,818 of qualified distribution, as seen in figure 16.2, with a $9,818 Roth distribution, as seen in figure 16.3.

The individual's total income remains the same; however, taxable income decreases 20.7 percent, from $77,370 (in figure 16.2) to $61,388 (in figure 16.3). The decrease in taxable income represents $15,982 annually. Assuming the individual is at a 20 percent effective tax rate (tax paid divided by adjusted gross income), the individual will save $3,196 in taxes annually. Although this may not sound like a lot of money, over twenty years, the savings would be $63,928, which could be spent as desired instead of spent on income tax.

The following figure 16.4 illustrates case study 5.3, as presented in chapter 5. The individual is a high-income earner who believed in the system and placed 100 percent of his retirement funds in qualified programs. The individual continues to work, receives a Social Security benefit, and is forced to take RMDs since he is older than 70½. Since the individual's Social Security is 85 percent taxable, the difference between his total and taxable income is $4,137, which represents the 15 percent portion of his Social Security benefit that is not taxable. Otherwise, every dollar this individual earns is 100 percent taxable. His situation looks like this:

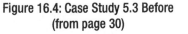

Figure 16.4: Case Study 5.3 Before (from page 30)   **Figure 16.5: Case Study 5.3 After**

| Total Income $333,927 | Taxable Income | Total Income $333,927 | Taxable Income |

In figure 16.4, the difference between total income and taxable income is $4,137, which represents 15 percent of the Social Security benefits and is not taxed.

In figure 16.5, qualified income, $213,252, minus Social Security, $4,137, plus interest earnings from non-qualified assets, $5,023, equals taxable income, $214,138.

If the individual had read *Positioning 4 Retirement* and followed its suggestions, things would have been different. Foreseeing that he might have a strong pension and receive a Social Security benefit, he might have contributed only the minimum to his employer-matching funds. If there was no match, he might have resisted contributing to qualified funds entirely and built a strong non-qualified portfolio.

Figure 16.5 presents this scenario, replacing qualified distributions with non-qualified. His total income would have stayed the same while his taxable income would have decreased $115,652, or 35 percent annually. Assuming a 20 percent effective tax rate, the individual would have protected $23,130 annually from paying income tax. Over twenty years, the individual would have avoided paying income tax on $2,313,040, of which $462,608 could have been used and enjoyed, instead of paying income tax.

Calculating State Income Tax Savings

Although *Positioning 4 Retirement* focuses on federal income tax, you can easily calculate the state income tax rate—both use the same method.

For example, in figures 16.2 and 16.3, if the calculated income is the same for state income tax purposes and the tax rate is 5 percent, by positioning income and assets as suggested, the individual would have saved $799 ($15,982 x 5 percent) annually and $15,980 over twenty years. The combined federal and state tax savings ($63,928 + $15,980) is $79,908 over twenty years.

In figures 16.4 and 16.5, using the same calculation process and tax rate as in the example above, the state income tax savings would be $5,783 ($115,652 x 5 percent) annually and $115,660 over twenty years. In this example, the combined federal and state tax savings would be $578,268 over twenty years.

Comparing the Four Graphs

Figures 16.2, 16.3, 16.4, and 16.5 present the effect qualified and non-qualified money can have on a retirement portfolio, income tax, and a wealthy, happy retirement. Most people in their retirement would rather spend their money on what they enjoy than on income tax.

Incomes as displayed in 16.3 are becoming more and more prevalent. What is considered a high-income earner today will be the average-income earner in thirty years, if not sooner. Some are already there. A thirty-year-old anticipating retiring at seventy years old is likely to build a retirement portfolio greater than what we have discussed. Strategic planning is essential.

CHAPTER 16 REVIEW QUESTIONS

Exploring Your Options

It is up to the individual to decide the direction he or she wants to follow by choosing what circumstances to have in retirement. The individual must also determine how to structure his or her retirement portfolio. Determining how each statement below applies to your situation will assist you in taking the proper steps for positioning for your retirement.

1. Accumulating qualified funds will place the tax burden on the individual during retirement.

   A. Important to me.
   B. Not important to me.
   C. Doesn't matter to me.

2. Accumulating non-qualified and Roth funds places the tax burden on the individual during the accumulation phase.

   A. Important to me.
   B. Not important to me.
   C. Doesn't matter to me.

3. By accumulating non-qualified funds during the accumulation phase, funds can be accessed for emergencies.

   A. Important to me.
   B. Not important to me.
   C. Doesn't matter to me.

4. By accumulating non-qualified funds during the accumulation phase, funds can be used for vacations and home improvements.

   A. Important to me.
   B. Not important to me.
   C. Doesn't matter to me.

5. By accumulating non-qualified funds, the tax is not deferred and the tax is not creating growth.

    A. Important to me.
    B. Not important to me.
    C. Doesn't matter to me.

6. Accumulating qualified funds allows the deferred tax to grow within the account.

    A. Important to me.
    B. Not important to me.
    C. Doesn't matter to me.

7. Accumulating qualified funds creates a greater necessity for a long-term care insurance policy.

    A. Important to me.
    B. Not important to me.
    C. Doesn't matter to me.

8. Accumulating mostly non-qualified funds allows me more options to protect wealth.

    A. Important to me.
    B. Not important to me.
    C. Doesn't matter to me.

9. If a life insurance policy is used to accumulate retirement funds and the insured passes away during the accumulation phase or shortly thereafter, there is a chance the beneficiaries will have a larger tax-free death proceed.

    A. Important to me.
    B. Not important to me.
    C. Doesn't matter to me.

10. If qualified funds are not protected, they will go toward long-term care expenses.

    A. Important to me.
    B. Not important to me.
    C. Doesn't matter to me.

11. When government rules and regulations change, there is less concern with non-qualified assets.

    A. Important to me.
    B. Not important to me.
    C. Doesn't matter to me.

12. Paying for long-term care by spending down assets is what is expected.

    A. Important to me.
    B. Not important to me.
    C. Doesn't matter to me.

There is no right or wrong answer to each statement in this review. Instead, the answers can assist you to in shaping the retirement of your choice.

Practical Application V

Now that you have read section 5, let's put things in perspective for you and your own situation.

1. Do you have long-term care insurance?

Print out and complete:

WS 23 Long-term Care Insurance Policies

Move the information to the spreadsheet.

2. List your legal documents

Print out and complete:

WS 24 Legal Documents

Move the information to the spreadsheet.

3. Ask yourself the following questions:

- Is spending down assets a concern for providing long-term care?
- Are you concerned with running out of money during retirement?
- Have you adequately protected yourself and your family against financial disaster and long-term care needs?
- What will your tax liability be when you retire?
- Have you done everything to minimize your tax liability for when you retire?

By now, you should have completed all worksheets from **www. Positioning4Retirement.com** that pertain to your funds and transferred the specified numbers to the spreadsheet. (There are twenty-five worksheets in total, but not all necessarily apply to your individual situation.) If you have not filled out your worksheets and spreadsheet, please return to the previous practical applications and do so now, referring to the appropriate chapters for assistance if needed. Completing these forms will help you manage and track your progress.

What You Will Need to Move Forward

CHAPTER 17

Building a Team
of Professionals

*Positioning 4 Retiremen*t is a book written to be easy to read and understand; however, the subject can be complex. Oftentimes, it is beneficial and cost effective to seek assistance. Building a team of professionals is essential in order to build a comprehensive retirement plan. The best time to begin assembling a team is based on individual circumstances. As assets accumulate, the team should begin to form consisting of the following four professionals: an estate and elder law attorney, a CPA focused on tax planning, an investment advisor, and an insurance professional. Communication among your team is essential. If there is no communication, there is no team!

Working with a team who already does business together ensures a level of beneficial chemistry and frequent communication. Team chemistry is very important. Ask a professional whom you are comfortable with if he or she can recommend other professionals to add to your team.

Your team of professionals works like a football team:

- The attorney represents the quarterback. As the one who leads and orchestrates each play, the attorney tells the other team members what actions should be taken at each phase.

- The CPA helps write the playbook, examining and positioning each play to maximize potential and minimize tax consequences.
- The offense is played by the investment professional who moves the plan forward, preserving and growing assets.
- The insurance professional plays defense, protecting and creating conservative advances. The team compares and cross-references plans and programs, creating a checks-and-balances system.
- You are the team owner—the one who makes decisions, directs the team as to where you want to go by communicating your needs, obligations, and objectives.

Separate the Financial Professionals and Double the Potential

It is advantageous to separate the financial retirement portfolio between an investment advisor and an insurance professional. Certain insurance and investment plans tend to overlap. It is virtually impossible for one individual to comprehend and stay on top of every program, product, and change that takes place on a daily basis. He or she is unable to maintain control of a person's investment portfolio and be 100 percent effective in all areas of the markets and the insurance industry. Therefore, the professional maintaining the investment portion of the financial portfolio should be focused on market-driven funds. The insurance professional should be focused on insurance-driven programs that are designed to protect assets from financial devastation, ultimately capturing and protecting the individual's wealth for retirement and heirs. The two professionals should be coordinated with your help and/or the assistance of your attorney and CPA. Communication amongst your professionals is key!

Another important point to know is there are three classifications of investment and insurance agents. You should be aware of the difference between them when selecting your investment and insurance professionals.

- **A captive agent** works within a limited product line. This person offers products only under his or her company's umbrella.
- **An affiliated agent** works under an umbrella network with a select group of companies chosen by the company holding the umbrella and is able to venture outside the umbrella for additional programs.
- **An independent agent** works as a representative to an investment or insurance company and has many insurance companies at his or her disposal, creating a bigger competitive environment.

Separating the investment and insurance professionals doubles the attention on your retirement portfolio. With the attention of a CPA and an estate planning attorney working for you, this tactic creates a retirement team that leads you to your ultimate objective: a comprehensive retirement portfolio.

Oftentimes, the client is concerned with the cost of having to pay the fees of these professionals. Once the process is complete, the client realizes the importance of assembling a team and how the benefits outweigh the costs.

Getting the Team Together in One Room

A big mistake people make when organizing their retirement and estate plan is not bringing their team of professionals together. It is encouraged to assemble them as each professional phase develops. Allowing your team of professionals to communicate will maximize your estate in all areas. Providing your thoughts, ideas, and objectives will help them to meet these goals. After all, they have no knowledge of what is going on in your life until you tell them. Bringing your team together and coordinating your legal, tax, and financial objectives will create a think tank; each member can focus and create a checks-and-balances system amongst the team. Assembling the team in one room allows them to brainstorm and come up with situations to benefit you.

Building a Retirement Portfolio

Structuring programs and plans is essential to a healthy portfolio A healthy portfolio minimizes tax and optimizes legal and financial options.

Many people ignore their retirement portfolio during the accumulation phase for various reasons—they have no time, it is not a priority, they do not understand it, they do not care to deal with it, etc. Meeting with your team once a year will prove to be beneficial for monitoring growth, positioning of assets, and educating you in these areas.

One of the biggest mistakes people make is waiting to organize their portfolio until they retire and allowing their accumulated funds to dictate their lifestyle after retirement.

At that point, they are adjusting their lifestyle to accommodate their income, as opposed to building an income to meet their desired retirement lifestyle. Most people are concerned with the gains and losses of retirement funds, as opposed to how they are positioned. By organizing and positioning retirement programs, you will be in control of your retirement.

Recognizing Inheritable Generational Wealth

Although you may not currently have protectable assets, you may inherit them. Certain programs, such as life insurance, are better established when a person is younger.

Case Study 17.1

Several years ago, I met with a woman in her early forties who was panicked. Her father, healthy and in his seventies, had met with his CPA. The week before we met, she was informed that she would be receiving several million dollars, as well as several properties when her father passes away. She knew her father was successful in business but did not realize the extent of his success. Her father suggested that she plan accordingly.

Fortunately, she was also healthy, and her father was willing to help her purchase insurance policies that would accommodate her future inheritance. We assembled a team of professionals that she was comfortable with and put the necessary legal and insurance programs in place to protect the assets for her and her family while also minimizing tax issues.

Assembling a team benefited not only her, but also her father and his grandchildren. Her father recognized the importance of accommodating the estate tax, how the tax would have affected his family, and what he had worked hard to achieve. He acted appropriately and responsibly. He understood that with wealth comes the responsibility to protect it.

Organizing Your Estate Plan

For people aged forty through eighty, organizing a team of professionals becomes a necessity if not already put into place—that is, unless you plan on winging it. Your team should be able to follow you through your golden years. This is why many estate planning attorneys also practice elder law; estate planning and elder law go hand in hand.

Choosing when to assemble your team will determine how well they will perform for you, so the earlier you do this, the better. Protecting your assets and providing your family with resources from issues that may come up in the future can be favorable to your family. Full disclosure of family dynamics is important to your team, especially to your attorney if you have a blended marriage, a disabled child, a child in a relationship that makes you uncomfortable, discord with a family member, prior marital arrangements such as divorces, etc.

For More Information

Article 9, "Team Planning Your Retirement and Your Estate," at the end of this book provides more detail on team building.

CHAPTER 17 REVIEW QUESTIONS

1. It is recommended to have a team of professionals to help assemble a retirement plan. The team would consist of an attorney and a CPA as fiduciaries and:

   A. A financial professional that does both investments and insurances.
   B. Separate investment and insurance professionals creating more focused attention to your retirement plan.
   C. It doesn't matter.

2. The biggest mistake people make, other than never putting together a team, is waiting until they retire to organize and position themselves. Waiting results in having to adjust their lifestyle to meet retirement income, rather than growing and planning their income to meet their retirement income expectations.

   TRUE　　FALSE

3. Getting the team to communicate and assembling them in one room has proven to be valuable.

   TRUE　　FALSE

4. Generational inherited wealth is not a concern when organizing your estate and should not be considered.

   TRUE　　FALSE

Answers: 1. B, 2. TRUE, 3. TRUE, 4. FALSE

CHAPTER 18

Conclusion: Now the Responsibility Is Yours!

A comprehensive retirement portfolio consists of an estate and tax plan that is coordinated with a financial plan. Monitoring your retirement portfolio involves time and attention. A financial plan requires us to balance and protect our principal and appreciation as they grow.

The insurance portfolio protects your retirement portfolio from financial upset, disaster, disability, and devastation, and most important, it protects your family from consequences that are created by these obstacles. Coordinating your insurance portfolio with your overall investment portfolio's growth, positioning assets and insurances in legal documents, managing income tax to your benefit, and combining all areas under one plan will optimize your retirement.

Accumulating wealth using this strategy can create an even and steady flow when entering the distribution phase; taking from the proper funds in a difficult market will create an even tax flow between qualified and non-qualified funds, maximizing Social Security benefits, and ultimately optimizing your retirement plan.

Proper rest is another key element for optimizing your retirement portfolio. Allowing the more challenged funds to rest and settle down in a dangerous market allows your funds to regroup, re-energize, and prepare to grow stronger.

Our objective when accumulating retirement funds is to prepare ourselves so we can live a long and healthy financial lifestyle. Most people accumulate these funds in order to secure a safe, happy, and long retirement and to pass their wealth on to their family, but they forget to protect it legally and with the proper insurance programs.

A well-diversified portfolio with a properly structured estate and tax plan allows you to live a long life without having to look back, knowing that your money will not run out and that your wishes will be honored when you die.

Now that you have read *Positioning 4 Retirement*, you should have:

- a better understanding of how to position retirement assets more effectively;
- an understanding as to the government's position in regards to retirement funds;
- an idea of the options available to balance qualified plans, offsetting government rules and regulations;
- a sense of comfort knowing you are in control of your retirement if you follow our suggestions.

Now it's in your hands! You have the chance to protect your hard-earned funds, remove the risks, and minimize tax exposure. It's your choice, it's your money, and it's now your responsibility!

What are you going to do?

Practical Application VI

To prepare adequately for your future and, if desired, provide for your heirs, you need to assemble a team of professionals. If you answer no to any of the following questions, **www.Positioning4Retirement.com** is here to help you find the professionals you may need. It is our objective to provide you with qualified professionals in your state. Please visit **www.Positioning4Retirement.com** and click on "Find a Professional." If there is no one listed in your area, print out "Choosing Your Team Professional" under the each category so you can personally qualify them.

1. **Do you have an attorney that specializes in estate and Medicaid planning?**

    ____Yes.   Complete worksheet WS 25, Team Professionals.
    ____No.   Proceed to the website to "Find a Professional."

2. **Do you have a CPA (not to be confused with a tax preparer)?**

    ____Yes.   Complete worksheet WS 25, Team Professionals.
    ____No.   Proceed to the website to "Find a Professional."

3. **Do you have an insurance professional who is experienced with estate and Medicaid planning, as well as retirement planning?**

    ____Yes.   Complete worksheet WS 25, Team Professionals.
    ____No.   Proceed to the website to "Find a Professional."

4. **Do you have a securities professional?**

    ____Yes.   Complete worksheet WS 25, Team Professionals.
    ____No.   Proceed to the website to "Find a Professional."

5. **Are the insurance and securities professionals the same person? If two different individuals, do they work in the same firm?**

    ____One person
    ____Two individuals in one firm
    ____Two individuals in two different firms

    It is suggested that they be separate individuals and work in separate firms.

6. Have you ever assembled your attorney, CPA, insurance, and securities professionals together to discuss your intentions?

    ____Yes.   Great!
    ____No.   It is suggested you do so.

7. On a scale of 1 to 10 with 10 being the best and 1 the worst, how would you rate the health of your retirement portfolio in these categories?

    ____Legally
    ____Tax wise
    ____Insurances
    ____Investments

    Your results should determine your comfort level. If you have less than 8 in any category, you may want to consider making a change.

ARTICLES BY MARK S. CARDOZA

The following nine articles offer more detailed information
on the topics and present specific opportunities
for planning for your retirement.

What Few Know about Their 401(k) and Other Qualified Retirement Funds

A different perspective on qualified money

This article is written for those who would like to learn more about qualified and non-qualified funds. It presents the popular, well-known attributes and exposes the unknown effects that qualified funds can have on retirement and estate planning. Here, "qualified" and "non-qualified" are defined in the conventional sense, but qualified money also has an unconventional definition that is important in understanding how qualified funds truly can affect your estate plan.

Before we go further, let's set the foundation and develop an understanding of what non-qualified money is. The conventional understanding of non-qualified money is:

- The principal funds have been taxed.
- Future interest growth on the principal is not always deferred.
- It can be held as cash, certificates of deposit, investments, part of a savings or checking account, life insurance, and/or annuities.
- This money can be used to pay your bills, buy groceries, pay for emergencies, go on vacations, etc.

When accessing information about qualified and non-qualified retirement funds and their uses, there is little information that references their position and effect in an estate plan.

Although this article does not focus on non-qualified money, it does present the relationship between non-qualified and qualified money. The primary intent is to expose the unknown aspects, the unconventional definition, and the function of qualified money.

The conventional understanding of qualified generally refers to programs named after their IRS code: 401(k), 403(b), 457(b), Roth, SEP, SIMPLE, TSA, and IRA. Within this definition:

- Principal contributions have not been taxed (with the exception of a Roth plan).
- Principal and interest grow tax-free until withdrawn.
- Upon withdrawal, the principal and growth are taxed, based on tax status at that time (with the exception of a Roth plan).
- Premature withdrawals (prior to age 59½), excluding special exceptions, are penalized.

Known to few, the unconventional, comprehensive understanding of qualified funds is everything as stated above, with the addition of the following:

Qualified status follows the guidelines and directives set by the IRS, enabling the intervention of the US government to control these funds, keeping the government's interests in mind, whether intentional or not. Qualified funds are subject to tax code changes and changes in government mandates by the IRS, US Treasury, and the US Congress.

The comprehensive definition of qualified funds is the diabolical reality behind a retirement plan. Few people know how this definition can affect their tax and estate planning during retirement. The government does an exceptional job of controlling your money for purposes you do not expect.

How Does This Affect You?

In most circumstances, when an individual or a couple retire, they begin to think about securing their estate for their heirs if they have not already done so. They generally do not discover the unconventional part of this explanation of qualified funds until they retire and are presented with the need for long-term care or in the event of their death(s).

For some reason, this information has been ignored, and when confronted, it is too late to correct it. The conveyance of this information has flown under the radar with most, though not all, financial professionals.

Most people plan to pass their hard-earned funds to their heirs, not to the government. The way qualified funds are mandated can curtail this intention.

A major concern is that many people make additional contributions above employee matching funds to a qualified retirement plan, playing right into the hands of the government simply because they are unaware of the potential threat. Why?

Based on information provided by the Employee Benefit Research Institute (EBRI), guidelines, mandates, and laws around retirement planning are made by politicians and big businesses. The government gets involved because we receive tax considerations by utilizing these plans. This is what is emphasized.

Do the Positives Outweigh the Negatives?

Consider these points.

- Positive: Our money grows tax deferred, compounding until we decide to take it out.
- Positive: When we take it out determines how much tax we pay.
- Negative: Excluding special circumstances, a 10 percent IRS penalty applies for premature withdrawal.

Two positives and only one negative: it sounds great. But is it?
Look at it this way:

- We mix our retirement funds with government funds by not paying income tax when funds are earned, deferring the tax, allowing what we would pay in tax to grow with the principal.
- The funds that went untaxed when they were earned or deferred are, in part, government funds (the tax portion).
- Over the years, stirring the money together, adding and subtracting growth, adapting to government policy, mandates, and guideline changes, and combining the principal with interest growth and losses creates a confused environment.
- We pay the taxes when we take it out based on the rules of the government (IRS), which can change at any time.
- Funds are held hostage with penalties; the funds cannot be used until the individual is 59½ and must begin to be taken no later than age 70½ to avoid penalties.

Required Minimum Distribution—RMD

Once a person reaches age 70½, IRS regulation mandates that qualified funds begin the distribution process if they have not already started. The calculation of a published Uniform Distribution Table based on the Uniform Lifetime Table (IRS Publication 590) determines the required minimum distribution, or RMD. If the RMD is not taken, then 50 percent of the remaining RMD from that year is applied as a penalty at tax time. As you grow older, the dividing factor in the equation decreases, which ultimately increases the required distribution and can potentially create more taxable income.

Upon the death of spouse, it is likely that the surviving spouse will inherit the decedent's qualified programs. This can have a major impact on taxability.

Case Study A1
Effects of an Inherited RMD

Two spouses are each the same age and each with $100,000 of qualified funds. At the end of each year, they will take their RMD. Their funds are growing an average of 3 percent annually. The chart below illustrates what they can expect.

Age	Beginning Value	Growth (3%)	Value	Divisor	RMD	Year End Balance	Percent RMD/Value
70½	100,000	3,000	103,000	27.4	3,759	99,241	3.65
71	99,241	2,977	102,218	26.5	3,857	98,361	3.77
72	98,361	2,951	101,312	25.6	3,958	97,354	3.91
73	97,354	2,921	100,275	24.7	4,060	96,215	4.05
74	96,215	2,886	99,101	23.8	4,164	94,937	4.20
75	94,937	2,848	97,785	22.9	4,270	93,515	4.30
76	93,515	2,805	96,320	22.0	4,378	91,942	4.54
77	91,942	2,758	94,700	21.2	4,467	90,233	4.72
78	90,233	2,707	92,940	20.3	4,578	88,362	4.93
79	88,362	2,651	91,013	19.5	4,667	86,346	5.13
80	86,346	2,590	88,936	18.7	4,756	84,180	5.35
81	84,180	2,525	86,705	17.9	4,844	81,861	5.59

One spouse passes away at age eighty-one leaving his fund to the surviving spouse. The RMD changes are as follows (the beginning value, or $163,722, is the year-end balance of $81,861 doubled for the surviving spouse):

Age	Beginning Value	Growth	Value	Divisor	RMD	Year End Balance	Percent
82	163,722	4,912	168,634	17.1	9,862	158,772	5.85
83	158,772	4,763	163,485	16.3	10,030	153,455	6.14
84	153,455	4,604	158,059	15.5	10,197	147,862	6.45
85	147,862	4,436	152,298	14.8	10,290	142,008	6.76

As presented, RMD continues to increase with age due to the divisor decreasing. Taxability can possibly double. Not only is taxability affected, but also, since this fund is qualified, the program(s) the funds are in must remain in the individual's name and Social Security number and, therefore, cannot be protected from the use for long-term care. If long-term care is needed, this fund would need to be spent down to $2,000 before Medicaid will step in.

The Overall Effect

Simply put, the government has a stake in qualified retirement plans and, therefore, has control over when those funds can be used, as well as how and when the US government can use it. More specifically, the government does the following:

- The government controls the amount we can contribute to a retirement plan.
- The government controls when we can begin using it and when we must begin using it.
- The government allows us to access our own money on their terms for special circumstances.
- The government puts minimum requirements for distribution on us or we pay a penalty.
- The government sets the rules we have to follow while establishing their own rules and has the authority to change the rules on both sides at any time.
- **Most important, the government keeps you from protecting qualified money for your family and heirs against long-term care needs. This is the biggest, most powerful, and most expensive threat retirees face and the one that's NOT talked about.**

Qualified money is vulnerable and accessible to Medicaid/nursing homes, as well as Social Security and qualified pension plans. There is only one legal document that will protect qualified money from being used for nursing home care: an IRS qualified retirement trust. This document makes the funds available to you during your lifetime and makes it available to future generations only after your death. This is beneficial only if you do not need the money, but it places the tax burden on your family. When they use it, their income will likely be greater than yours; combining the assets will create a higher tax for them.

There are insurance programs that will help protect qualified funds, such as a long-term care insurance (LTCI), life insurance programs, and annuities that are designed with LTCI needs in mind. An LTCI policy protects your funds while allowing you to continue to use the money.

The EBRI reports that in 2003 an estimate of $1.9 trillion dollars in assets were held in 401(k) plans involving 43.3 million active participants. Although this is the most recent data available, imagine how large these numbers are now, several years after the information was published.

Why Can't I Put My Qualified Money in a Trust That Allows Me to Use My Money before I Die?

Qualified funds must be kept in the individual's Social Security number instead of a separate entity with its own tax ID. Therefore, qualified money cannot be placed in a legal document such as a trust, unless tax is paid so that the funds become non-qualified. Non-qualified funds can be protected in a trust with its own tax identification number, creating a separate entity. However, this defeats the purpose of placing the money in a qualified fund and then taking the funds at an assumed lower tax rate during retirement.

What Happens to My Qualified Money When I Die?

You have several options for what will happen to your money upon your death.

1. Qualified funds can be transferred to the spouse upon death; however, the transfer must be made into the surviving spouse's name and his or her Social Security number. This creates another tax issue as presented below under "Typical Situations."

2. Qualified funds can also be transferred to a child, grandchild, or sibling, based on the guidelines set under the Pension Protection Act of 2006 (PPA'06) and IRS Notice 2008-30. In order to do this, you must meet the criteria and follow the IRS rules. This allows you to continue the tax deferred status and allows the government to utilize the funds in the event that your beneficiary needs Medicaid assistance. The funds continue to be unprotected and are unable to be protected.

3. When money is taken out of a qualified fund, the IRS and the individual are notified at tax time. The individual must treat the funds as ordinary income because he or she is taxed as such.

4. The objective is to pay taxes on the funds when your taxable income is assumed to be lower, such as during retirement. For example: during working life, a person may experience an effective tax rate of 25 percent. When retired, he or she would experience an effective

tax rate of 0–15 percent. Therefore, the accumulated qualified funds would be taxed at 0–15 percent. However, due to wealth accumulation, Social Security, pension, RMD, and changes in tax laws, many people are retiring and remaining in the same tax bracket as they were while they worked and, therefore, are not experiencing a substantially lower tax rate. In some circumstances, income and wealth have gone up while tax rates have gone down, putting taxpayers in a holding pattern.

Note: *Inherited generational wealth can create a great problem if it is not recognized and structured properly.*

Typical Situation

A married couple accumulates qualified funds while they are both alive and their tax deductions and brackets are proportionate. When one of them dies, the surviving spouse's deductions decrease by 50 percent after the first year, the tax bracket changes from married filing jointly to single, cutting the allowable taxable income in half, and his or her qualified funds are added together to create greater individual wealth. The RMD then increases due to the inheritance, and the divisor continues to decrease due to age, creating a potential tax liability. Social Security is then recalculated based on individual circumstances.

Tax is not the only concern. Remember that qualified funds cannot be protected. In the event that long-term care is needed, everything is absorbed before Medicaid steps in, with the exception of $2,000—the current allowable asset limit an individual can retain. If the couple contributed 100 percent into a qualified plan, it is likely they will forfeit 100 percent of their remaining retirement funds to their long-term care needs before Medicaid. Also, if there are any non-qualified funds that are not protected, they too will be used before Medicaid assistance.

Solution 1
Make contributions to a qualified plan equal to the amount that is being matched by your employer, **but no more**. If you plan to contribute more to a qualified plan, contribute with caution.

The Rule of 100 is a good tool to follow when considering the amount of risk to be taken at a particular age. The Rule of 100 recommends taking the number 100 and subtracting your age. The remaining number represents the percentage of assets that can be at risk. For example, if you are 45 years old, 100 - 45 = 55. Therefore 55 percent of your assets can be at risk, and 45 percent should be protected.

Your portfolio should be diversified utilizing:

- A qualified plan with contributions equal to your employer's match.
- A non-qualified plan, minimal risk to risk-free.
- Risk-based assets, referencing the Rule of 100, as shown above.
- A life insurance policy established as a retirement vehicle, as well as death benefits with accessibility to cash value while alive and upon death. The cash value in a life insurance policy works well in a down market, as discussed in article 6, "The Role of Life Insurance and Your Retirement Plan."
- A long-term care policy to protect all liquid assets (including qualified) and real property.
- The proper legal documents supporting the programs with respect to your wishes and your family situation.
- A strategic tax plan to minimize taxability and coordinate income in a down market, optimizing overall potential. Planning your tax exposure is a smart move—it puts you in control, taking charge of your retirement destiny.

By having less qualified funds and more non-qualified funds, RMD payouts are less threatening, and taxes can be coordinated and managed more efficiently to create a situation where qualified money dips below the qualified perimeter and is not taxed. Too much qualified money reacts the opposite way and creates a taxable situation.

Solution 2
Explore alternate ways of building retirement funds independent of qualified funds.

Everything in moderation ... too much of one thing is no good. There is nothing wrong with accumulating qualified funds, but for some unknown reason, our society has been driven to believe that accumulating qualified money is the best way to build for retirement. I call it the "Black Friday Syndrome." I often meet people who add extra money into their 401(k) each month because they believe it to be a great opportunity. People perceive this as the only way to achieve a safe and healthy retirement; but this is not always the case. Retirement funds can be accumulated using several methods that are separate from qualified funds.

Non-qualified Fixed Index Annuities

Open a separate and independent non-qualified retirement plan such as an annuity. An annuity, in many circumstances, is what your employer uses for his or her 401(k) and most likely has it set up as an employer-sponsored qualified plan.

Many plans will match each deposit 4–12 percent for several years. The matching bonus—up-front interest—is coming from the insurance company because this plan is independent. The money entering the fund is 100 percent yours, based on the terms of the contract, and has fewer government attachments since taxes have already been paid on these earnings. Interest growth in a non-qualified annuity grows tax deferred, just like in a qualified account without intervention. Tax on interest earned is paid upon withdrawal. Tax treatment of most tax deferred annuities are LIFO—last in, first out.

Guaranteed income riders are available on many annuities and enhance the growth substantially. Used to supplement Social Security, they are income streams for life. Certain annuities offer guarantees, such as downside protection, where principal and interest growth are locked in on each anniversary, as discussed in article 5, "Considering Fixed Index Annuities." Surrender periods can apply under certain circumstances with some annuities. Penalty-free withdrawals help to offset surrender charges.

Note: *The largest and most important difference within deferred annuities is the type of funds represented. If they are not qualified funds, the trust, not the individual, can be the owner and thus protected and built to your specific needs and requests.*

Annuities with Guaranteed Income Riders

In order to optimize your income potential, consider an income rider as an opportunity. Over the past ten years or so, insurance companies have been evolving to meet the needs of their contract holders and to offset the struggling economy while also creating ways to protect assets and preserve incomes. Income riders offer a guaranteed lifetime income to their contract holders.

Add this to an annuity that offers guarantees, such as downside protection, to make a total package. Protecting your money from downside risk while exposing it to upside potential is ideal. It ultimately guarantees that you can never lose your principal while locking in your growth upon the anniversary of your contract. Please reference article 5, "Considering Fixed Index Annuities."

Life Insurance Built for Income during Retirement

The right type of life insurance policy can play a huge role in an individual's overall retirement plan. Whole life or universal life policies allow for cash accumulation and various methods of growth. Not only can they grow like an annuity, but they also don't have the same restrictions as retirement plans.

Provided that the annual policy premium stays below the modified endowment contract (MEC) limitations, the 59½ rule does not apply to cash-value insurance policies. There are no restrictions on when you can take money out because the funds are non-qualified. Since a life insurance policy follows the first in, first out (FIFO) method, the first funds distributed are the premiums and are not taxable. The MEC is a cap that sets and limits the ability to accumulate cash value in a life insurance policy using the FIFO method. Premium deposits above the limit will create a MEC, which is irreversible and cash withdrawals are taxable.

Since life insurance proceeds and life insurance cash value are not taxed upon the death of the insured (provided the premiums were paid by an individual and not a corporation), the MEC prevents people from overfunding policies to avoid paying tax on the deferred gains.

Additional funds placed in a life insurance contract above the MEC create a taxable event when withdrawing funds prior to death. Certain life insurance policies are designed to secure retirement funds and coordinate with the MEC.

A MEC reverses the FIFO tax method to last in, first out (LIFO), causing the interest to be paid out first. Please reference article 6, "The Role of Life Insurance and Your Retirement Plan."

Combining, Coordinating, and Managing Qualified Funds

Social Security and pensions must be included when discussing the combination and coordination of qualified funds. Social Security may need an overhaul, and we should expect changes, but Social Security is beyond elimination.

Social Security and pension plans are considered qualified because taxes have not been paid on them. Therefore, they are not protected from the costs of long-term care needs. If you were to need long-term care and apply for Medicaid, your Social Security and pension would be redirected to the nursing facility, and a small portion would be allotted to you as an allowance. Allowances are different in each state.

Any qualified funds would be scrutinized, as well as any other unprotected assets, such as real estate and unprotected non-qualified funds. Remember, qualified funds must remain in the individual's Social Security number and cannot be protected. It is important not to be greedy when managing and coordinating qualified funds.

The EBRI reports that, in 2010, 8.5 percent of our population over age sixty-five lived in a nursing home. It also reports an increased use of long-term care insurance: 14 percent of entrants in 2010 had long-term care insurance. Therefore, 86 percent did not have insurance and either voluntarily paid down assets or were forced to privately pay (utilizing qualified retirement plans and other unprotected assets) before Medicaid.

Note: *It is important to keep in mind that, if you are accumulating qualified funds, a portion of those funds do not belong to you. Expect and plan to pay some tax on them. Plan to coordinate qualified funds with your Social Security benefit and pension. Failure to involve the necessary professional can be more costly than his or her fees.*

Put together a plan to work down your qualified funds and make them non-qualified so they can be protected. This is a method that allows you to be in control and to determine how much tax you are going to pay. The best way to do this is to meet with your accountant, your estate planning attorney, your insurance professional, and your securities advisor. Reference article 9, "Team Planning Your Retirement and Your Estate."

Protecting Your Qualified Funds

Let's discuss a way to protect your qualified funds and keep the government from using them to care for you if you need long-term care. There is a group of people with strong wealth who can endure the cost of long-term care if needed. They are self-insuring and often choose not to purchase long-term care insurance. It is imperative for those who have put a large portion of their retirement funds into qualified funds to look into some form of long-term care insurance. Each of the options is discussed in article 8, "The Role of Long-term Care Insurance and Your Retirement Plan."

This brings up a question I often hear: What if I never need to go into a nursing home and my family takes care of me at home?

When you are dealing with the unknown, it is recommended that you plan for the worst. Many policies provide for home health care. If the policy is a shared plan, then it will preserve the policy for the spouse. If it is a life insurance policy with a rider or endorsement, then it will provide a tax-free death benefit for your family when you die. Today, information is being released that recognizes home health care and assisted living as more prevalent than nursing home care. Thus, the term "extended care" is becoming more popular, encompassing home health care and assisted living as separate from nursing home care. Nursing homes, synonymous with skilled nursing facilities, are calling themselves "transitional care" because they realize that most people stay in these facilities for a short period of time and are then transferred to their home.

It is important to investigate comprehensive long-term care insurance plans that can be used for both phases. This topic is discussed in depth in article 8, "The Role of Long-term Care Insurance and Your Retirement Plan."

Who Is Responsible: You or the US Government?

The US government should present all the information pertaining to qualified assets, both positive and negative. Providing this information will allow individuals to make clear, well-informed decisions when planning for retirement. But they don't! In reality, the government recognizes the issues and offers us citizens the opportunity to protect ourselves.

- The government has given us the opportunity to position our assets into a legal document, such as an IRS qualified trust, to protect those assets for our heirs.
- The government allows us to use multiple vehicles to accumulate funds that are not only safe but also provide a friendly shelter for money without government intervention, such as annuities and life insurance.
- The government understands the need and versatility for long-term care insurance and offers a potential tax deduction that is given to those who have long-term care insurance for individuals and corporations.

The government, with all its politicians and influential corporate CEOs, has provided us with the necessary tools to protect ourselves. It is up to us to learn about them and take advantage of them. Now, after reading this article and the others recommended:

- Are you more aware of the dangers of qualified money?
- What are you going to do?

The responsibility is on you!

Social Security Benefits and Options for Retirement

It is not always clear when one should take Social Security benefits. Affordability, health issues, and the death of a spouse can eliminate this question for those who need this income to meet their everyday obligations during retirement. Here are highlights about Social Security:

- You, your spouse, or ex-spouse (if still unmarried) must contribute to the system in order to receive a retirement benefit. Individuals born after 1928 must contribute forty working calendar quarters (ten years) of credits to qualify.
- It is anticipated that individuals will need 70 to 80 percent of their pre-retirement income to live comfortably during retirement. For the average worker, Social Security replaces approximately 40 percent of their income.
- The Social Security benefit is based on a credit system. In 2014, $1,200 equaled one credit. The benefit is calculated from the highest thirty-five years of salary history.
- Full retirement age is based on the year you were born. The chart, "How Social Security Benefits Are Determined," is located in chapter 4. Regardless of full retirement age, you should enroll for Medicare three months prior to your sixty-fifth birthday.
- You do not need to contribute directly to the Social Security system in order to receive Medicare benefits. You can receive benefits through a spouse, deceased spouse, or ex-spouse, provided he or she has adequately contributed to the system or paid Medicare payroll

tax. If none of these criteria has been achieved, it will be reflected in the premium. The premium is based on the number of credits accumulated by the Social Security Administration. A person with no credits would pay the maximum premiums.

- Benefits can start as early as sixty-two years old, although benefits are reduced from full retirement age based on the year you are born.
- Benefits can be delayed indefinitely; although, most people delay no longer than age seventy.
- Currently, benefits grow approximately 8 percent annually. This is called "delayed retirement credits," and it begins once full retirement age is reached. The credits are calculated monthly until seventy years old.
- The maximum allowable benefit in 2014 was $2,642. In order for an individual to receive the maximum benefit, he or she will have contributed the maximum amount for thirty-five years.
- A cost-of-living adjustment (COLA) will apply once a benefit is opened. The COLA is based on the consumer price index and must be approved by Congress.
- Each month, Social Security pays the benefit for the previous month. They do not pay a benefit for the month in which the individual dies.
- Upon the death of an individual, the Social Security benefit received for that month must be returned into the system. Example: A person receives his benefit on the third of each month and dies on the last day of the month. The benefit that will be sent out for that month must be returned.
- Spouses that have never worked or have low earnings can be eligible to receive up to half of their spouse's benefit.
- Social Security is taxable.
- Special incomes, such as bonuses, vacation pay, commissions, and sick pay, should not affect your Social Security benefit because the income was generated prior to retirement.
- Military service members can receive full Social Security benefits, as well as a military pension. Extra credits are added to members of the military under certain circumstances.
- Family benefits range from spouses, ex-spouses, children up to nineteen years old, disabled children starting at eighteen years old, and unwed children over eighteen years old.
- Upon the death of a spouse, Social Security will pay a surviving spouse benefit, provided that they were married for no less than nine months and meet other criteria.

- Disabled widows or widowers can receive benefits as early as fifty years old and can update their benefit at full retirement age and receive full benefit.
- Upon the death of a spouse, the surviving spouse can receive the greater benefit.
- Individuals that pay into the Social Security system and a pension program are able to receive benefits from both plans. However, if the pension is provided by the government (federal, state, and/or local) and there were no contributions into the Social Security system, then the Social Securitybenefit can be reduced.
- Upon the death of an individual, Social Security will send the surviving spouse or a qualified family member $255.
- Individuals employed by Social Security are not advisors.
- Social Security guidelines can change with little notice.

Social Security Can Get Complicated and Confusing

Individuals that continue working and delay their benefits have many options to consider, especially if they have a spouse. Widowed and divorced-unmarried spouses and dependent children have opportunities as well.

For individuals that have been single their whole life, Social Security is very simple and easy to understand. The choices are three: receive a reduced benefit early, receive a benefit at full retirement age, or delay the benefit.

For individuals and married couples that retire out of necessity, retire with an illness, or receive their benefit due to an employment situation, the decision is obvious. Some people take their benefit early because they can't financially or physically afford not to begin receiving Social Security.

Benefits are based on a person's birth date, gender, and life expectancy. Life expectancy is established by the government and published on a chart that can change at any time. Currently, the average life expectancy for a sixty-five-year-old male is eighty-four, and a woman's life expectancy is eighty-six. If an individual's full retirement age is sixty-five and if he or she begins receiving a benefit at age sixty-two, then the person will receive thirty-six months of benefits before full retirement age. If the individual delays the benefits until age seventy, then he or she fails to receive a benefit for sixty months. Based on the life expectancy chart, the individual will need to receive a larger benefit in order to have received equal benefit when he or she reaches age eighty-four/eighty-six. The total dollar value of a delayed benefit will match the total dollar value of a reduced benefit at age eighty-four/eighty-six. Therefore, individuals that delay their benefit until seventy years old and live beyond eighty-four/eighty-six will receive a greater overall benefit.

Social Security becomes complicated and confusing when individuals attempt to maximize their benefits by using features built into the system that were meant to accommodate spouses and individuals who are unsure of taking the leap into retirement. These benefit options became abused, forcing Social Security to consider adjusting their policies.

The Social Security Administration revised a policy in 2010 that reforms withdrawal and the option to open and close a benefit. The original purpose for this feature was to accommodate individuals that chose to leave retirement and return to work. Oftentimes, people decide to retire and become bored. Others retire due to a health condition but then recuperate and reenter the workforce. Withdrawal and delayed retirement allow those in similar situations to receive their Social Security benefit and then put it on hold by returning the benefit later on. Once they are ready to retire, they are able to reopen their account and receive the increased benefit.

For those born in 1943 or later, Social Security benefits grow monthly, averaging 8 percent annually. The benefit growth is calculated using the simple interest calculation method beginning at full retirement age until age seventy. Once the individual hits seventy, annual growth stops, and cost-of-living adjustments begin, based on congressional approval. Even though an individual can receive benefits at sixty-two, the system internally continues to calculate growth on the individual's file until age seventy. Prior to December 8, 2010, the individual could return his or her benefit without interest any time before age seventy and would receive the increased benefit as if a benefit had never been taken.

A media-driven financial tactic promoted this as an opportunity to receive an interest-free loan. At first glance it is very attractive; however, when you take into consideration the increased taxability, tax rates, the interest growth needed to generate and offset these changes, fees that may be associated with the investment strategy, and the changes in regulations, this tactic may not be beneficial.

Impact Analysis

A husband and wife, sixty-five and sixty-two, respectively, continue to work and choose to take their Social Security benefits for the unintended purpose. Together, their benefits are $3,500 monthly, or $42,000 annually. Their combined adjusted gross earnings without Social Security are $185,000. They are in the 30 percent tax bracket, and their effective tax rate is 18 percent. By taking their Social Security benefit, which is 85 percent taxable, they will increase their adjusted gross earnings to $220,700 (.85 x $42,000, or $35,700, plus $185,000), putting them in a higher tax bracket and increasing their effective tax rate to 21 percent.

With their effective tax rate increased from approximately 18 percent (on $185,000 where they paid $33,027 in taxes) to approximately 21 percent (on $220,700, where they paid $45,235 in taxes), their income tax increased by $12,208. To recoup this increase in tax from the addition of their Social Security benefits, their investments would need to be greater than $12,208. In reality, their Social Security after tax is $29,792, or $2,483 a month.

Practices such as this forced the Social Security Administration to take a new look at this opportunity. Based on a news release on December 8, 2010, the Social Security Administration published a new rule to take place immediately. The rule was reformed to:

limit the time period for beneficiaries to withdraw an application for retirement benefits to within 12 months of the first month of entitlement and to one withdrawal per lifetime. In addition, beneficiaries entitled to retirement benefits may voluntarily suspend benefits only for the months beginning after the month in which the request is made.

This means that individuals who are unclear as to whether they want to retire have a window of twelve months after they receive the benefit to decide to go back to work. Should an individual decide to return to work, he or she chooses to suspend the benefit within that twelve-month period. Hoping to eradicate loopholes, the Social Security Administration made this option available only one time. The new rule was enacted immediately so that those who were taking advantage of the system were unable to receive an increased benefit.

Every situation is different. Do your homework and analyze how this tactic and other tactics will affect your situation. Consult your team of professionals.

Spouses' Benefits

Family dynamics, pensions, and spousal benefits may complicate the options that are available to married couples. Before discussing these options, let's understand the fundamentals of spouses' benefits.

Spousal benefits are designed for spouses and ex-spouses that either never worked or earned low wages. The spouse can receive up to 50 percent of the working spouse's benefits once the non-working spouse has reached full retirement age. The situation becomes confusing when different family dynamics are incorporated, such as spouses that begin a career late in life or marriages that end in death or divorce.

The best way to understand your options is to meet with a representative from Social Security. Keep in mind that although Social Security representatives are helpful and knowledgeable, they are not there to advise you; the representative will calculate the benefit of an option that you present. With this information, couples that choose to continue working after their full retirement age have opportunities to maximize their benefits. This opportunity is referred to as "file and suspend" or "restricted application."

Spousal Benefits Using Suspend and Restrict and Their Differences

Both suspend and restrict are opportunities for married couples. Suspend allows a spouse to receive an additional benefit based on the working spouse's benefit. This process enhances the non-working spouse's benefit until the working spouse retires. Restrict allows a working spouse to receive a benefit based on his or her retired spouse's benefit. Suspend and restrict are opportunities for married couples to delay and fortify the benefits of one spouse. It is perfectly legal but may be under the scrutiny of the Social Security Administration.

Suspend
At full retirement age, one spouse decides to continue working while the other spouse retires. The spouse that continues to work files for his or her Social Security benefit and requests to have the payments suspended. This will enable:

- the working spouses to delay his or her benefit, which allows it to continue growing;
- the second spouse to retire at age sixty-two, with an opportunity for a spouses' benefits in addition to his or her own.

Once the working spouse retires, his or her benefit will be larger because it will have been delayed. At that point, the spousal benefit that the retired spouse was receiving will be eliminated.

Restrict
Restricting an application is a strategy used to maximize Social Security benefits for a working spouse because he or she can collect a spousal benefit while delaying his or her own. It generally works best when both spouses are relatively close in age and one is planning to work beyond full retirement age. Once both spouses have reached full retirement age:

- one spouse can retire and take his or her benefit, and the other spouse can continue to work;
- the working spouse files his or her Social Security application, restricting it to spousal benefits, and can receive a spousal benefit.

This will allow the working spouse to delay his or her benefit, receiving a larger benefit upon retirement while also receiving a spousal benefit until that time. There is a very small window of opportunity here because full retirement age is between sixty-five and sixty-seven and the maximum benefit is reached at age seventy.

Ex-spouse Benefits from Divorce, Annulment, or Death

A former spouse by divorce, annulment, or death is able to take advantage of these strategies provided he or she meets certain qualifications. The former spouse must have been married for at least ten years and, based on what he or she is filing, must be at least of retirement age and unmarried. Benefits are available even if the former spouse is not retired, provided that the age requirement is met.

If you, the working spouse, have remarried, the benefit your ex-spouse receives has no effect on the benefits you and your current spouse can receive. You have no need to know your ex-spouse has filed for a benefit or is receiving a benefit; an ex-spouse has no need to inform you he or she is receiving a benefit based on your filing.

An ex-spouse due to death has benefits available to him or her provided the situation meets the criteria set by the Social Security Administration.

Risk Factors

If an individual decides to use any of these strategies, then he or she should be wary of potential risk.

There are tax ramifications. These strategies can change your Social Security tax formula and adjusted gross earnings. If the change sends you above the threshold, then it could make your income taxable, and your Social Security benefit could go from 0 taxability to 50 percent taxable. If you are at 50 percent, then the added income could push you into the 85 percent category. These changes in tax reporting can have a negative impact on your tax bracket and effective tax rate. The Social Security Administration can change its rules with very little or no notice. If that were to happen, then the benefits can get locked in at a lower level than planned.

Roth Plans

A Roth is a retirement program that has special tax considerations. There are two types of Roth plans, or programs: an employer-designated Roth and a Roth IRA. Both types accept contributions up to their respective limits, and contributions can be made to either plan independently of the other.

Under both Roth programs, the funds contributed to the plan are non-qualified and, therefore, have been taxed; however, Roth plans follow the guidelines of qualified plans and are classified as "qualified." By placing funds into a Roth account, non-qualified funds become qualified. Roth plans can consist of stocks, bonds, mutual funds, CDs, and annuities.

The two types of Roth programs have the following features.

1. **Designated Roth Account** is a program offered by some employers separate from 401(k), 403(b), or 457(b) programs. Like all Roth plans, contributions to the account grow tax free and remain tax free upon withdrawal. This type of plan will accept elected deferrals, also known as Roth contributions. It allows the individual to withdraw funds during retirement, provided the individual meets the requirements. However, not all employer-qualified plans offer a Roth option.

2. **Roth IRA** is an individual retirement account conducted outside your employer and through a bank, investment company, or insurance company. This account also accepts non-qualified money and turns it into qualified money, allowing it to grow tax free. A Roth IRA is also tax free upon withdrawal.

Roth Plans vs. Traditional Qualified Plans

In both types of Roth plans, the funds are added to the account after being taxed. A traditional qualified plan accepts funds before a tax has been applied. This is the difference between a traditional qualified plan and a Roth. The portion that would have been paid as tax grows with the principal in a traditional plan. Roth contributions have already been taxed, but future growth is tax free. Roth programs allow the individual to accumulate and withdraw his or her funds based on the criteria set by the IRS. When placing funds in a Roth plan, keep in mind the following:

- The individual must have an income-producing activity and receive a W-2 or 1099.
- Based on your income and filing status, contribution limits can change annually.
- The funds must remain in a Roth plan for a minimum of five years. The initial deposit begins the five-year period. Subsequent deposits do not have their own waiting period.
- The individual must be older than 59½ to withdraw funds to avoid a 10 percent penalty.

Participating in Both Roth Plans

To participate in either Roth plan, an individual (in 2014) must meet one of the following three criteria:

1. a single person or head of household with a modified adjusted gross income (AGI) of less than $114,000
2. head of household that is married filing separately (who did not live with his or her spouse) with modified AGI of less than $114,000
3. married couple filing jointly or qualifying widow(er) with a modified AGI of less than $181,000

It is important not to exceed the income limit because there is a 6 percent excise tax that is applied to excess Roth IRA contributions.

Provided the income criterion is met, an individual can maximize his or her designated Roth plan by contributing up to the allowable limit of $17,500 annually. Contributions are made through the designated employer-sponsored Roth.

Some 401(k), 403(b) SARSEP, and 457(b) allow catch-up contributions, and an individual can add an additional $5,500 if the individual is older than fifty years old. It is important to note that the income criteria are subject to annual change.

An individual can also open a Roth IRA and contribute $5,500. Once the individual reaches fifty years old, an additional $1,000 can be contributed annually on an individual basis. This is oftentimes referred to as a catch-up contribution.

Single people filing as head of household and earning from $114,000 to $129,000 can still contribute a percentage based on IRS worksheet 2-2 that will determine the amount allowable. Married couples filing jointly may contribute if they earn from $181,000 to $191,000 using the same worksheet.

Roth Plans and Required Minimum Distributions (RMDs)

Designated Roth accounts have RMDs that follow the same RMD guidelines as traditional qualified funds; however, there are no RMDs on a Roth IRA. Although RMDs must be taken at age 70½ with a designated Roth plan, there are no RMDs applicable to a Roth IRA. An individual is allowed to contribute into a Roth IRA after age 70½.

A Roth plan may provide income above and beyond the RMD of a traditional qualified plan, assisting to minimize taxable income and preserve Social Security taxability. In the event that you fail to take the full RMD—whether it is from a designated Roth or a qualified plan in any particular year—the portion that you did not take is 50 percent taxable.

Instead of withdrawing money from a qualified account, consider taking the funds from a Roth plan. There would be no effect on your taxable income if the money is taken from a Roth.

For more detailed information, please reference IRS Publications 590 and 575 or contact your CPA for specific questions regarding your situation.

The Power of a Roth

The hypothetical illustration viewed on page 161 uses a fixed index annuity, based on current contribution limits, the limit never changing, and a conservative average interest rate with no interest for nine years. (This example does not include fees, caps, spreads, charges, or participation rates.)

Over a period of thirty-eight years, the individual will have accumulated $489,236 and avoided down markets. In a less conservative market posing greater risk, the account may perform differently.

Based on an analysis using the history of the S&P 500 over a thirty-eight-year period, from 1976 to 2013, combining positive and negative years, the index performed an average rate of 12.93 percent.

Based on the illustration eliminating down markets as a fixed index annuity does, the index would have performed an average of 15.44 percent over the same thirty-eight years, a difference of 2.51 percent annually.

Example of the Power of a Roth IRA

At age twenty-nine, Mike works with others who neglected to accumulate for retirement when they were young and are now facing an adverse retirement plan. They are making their retirement lifestyle fit their retirement means with Social Security, a pension, and a small qualified plan. No one taught them how to plan for retirement. Because of them, Mike understands the need to begin accumulating for retirement as early as possible and is comfortable placing $12,000 a year into his retirement portfolio, as detailed in the following.

Mike's first decision is to form a team of professionals. Since he is young and has not accumulated many assets, he begins to develop a relationship with an insurance professional that has a team in place for him.

Mike will contribute to his employer-sponsored traditional qualified 401(k) plan up to its $3,000 matching limit, taking advantage of the company's generosity. Knowing he will be taxed when he withdraws money during retirement, Mike's contribution is no more than the $3,000 a year being matched by his employer.

His employer does not offer a designated Roth plan; however, since Mike currently meets the income criteria, he will contribute to a Roth IRA. If Mike stays below the income limits and opens a Roth IRA with an insurance company using a fixed index annuity, then the strategy is as follows:

1. Each year, Mike puts $5,500 into his IRA for twenty-one years until he is fifty years old. At age fifty, he has $115,500 principal plus compounding interest growth.
2. At age fifty, he contributes $6,500 annually for seventeen years until he retires at age sixty-seven for a contribution in this period of $110,500. Over the total thirty-eight years, Mike has contributed $226,000 in principal to his Roth IRA.

Since Mike chose to use a fixed index annuity for his Roth IRA, he can never lose the principal he contributed because it has downside protection. Mike also chose an annual point-to-point crediting method using the S&P 500. If Mike's plan grows an average of 5 percent annually with nine years that never perform, he calculates that he will have close to half a million dollars in tax-free money.

He can use as much as he wants whenever he wants without having to pay tax on the withdrawal. He can offset potential tax liability caused by his RMD from his traditional qualified plan. The funds can be reclassified as

Year	Age	Deposit	Interest: 5% of Deposit	Balance
1	29	$5,500	$275	$5,775
2	30	$5,500	$564	$11,839
3	31	$5,500	$867	$18,206
4	32	$5,500	0	$23,706
5	33	$5,500	$1,460	$30,666
6	34	$5,500	$1,808	$37,974
7	35	$5,500	$2,174	$45,648
8	36	$5,500	0	$51,148
9	37	$5,500	$2,832	$59,480
10	38	$5,500	$3,249	$68,229
11	39	$5,500	$3,686	$77,415
12	40	$5,500	0	$82,915
13	41	$5,500	$4,421	$92,836
14	42	$5,500	$4,917	$103,253
15	43	$5,500	$5,438	$114,191
16	44	$5,500	0	$119,691
17	45	$5,500	$6,260	$131,451
18	46	$5,500	$6,848	$143,799
19	47	$5,500	$7,465	$156,764
20	48	$5,500	0	$162,264
21	49	$5,500	$8,388	$176,152
22	50	$6,500	$9,133	$191,785
23	51	$6,500	$9,914	$208,199
24	52	$6,500	0	$214,699
25	53	$6,500	$11,060	$232,259
26	54	$6,500	$11,938	$250,697
27	55	$6,500	$12,860	$270,057
28	56	$6,500	0	$276,557
29	57	$6,500	$14,153	$297,210
30	58	$6,500	$15,186	$318,896
31	59	$6,500	$16,270	$341,666
32	60	$6,500	0	$348,166
33	61	$6,500	$17,733	$372,399
34	62	$6,500	$18,945	$397,844
35	63	$6,500	$20,217	$424,561
36	64	$6,500	0	$431,061
37	65	$6,500	$21,878	$459,439
38	66	$6,500	$23,297	$489,236
Total		$226,000	$263,236	

non-qualified by liquidating the accounts entirely or in part after age 59½ (provided the accounts are older than five years). If he turns his Roth IRA into non-qualified funds, Mike can place it in an irrevocable trust, protecting it for his heirs and moving it out of harm's way.

Although Mike currently meets the income limits for Roth plans, his personal goal is to exceed the limit, putting him in a situation where a Roth would not be available to him. Applying for a permanent cash-value life insurance policy that is used as a savings vehicle when his income reaches beyond the allowable Roth limits is the smart option. Mike understands that life insurance is based on age and health. Because he is young and healthy, this is a good time to minimize the cost for the future. His annual premium is $2,200.

Mike should also consider what would happen if he becomes disabled at any time in his life. His employer offers short- and long-term disability insurance that will help offset his income, supporting his household bills but not enough to compensate for the $12,000 he places in his retirement plan each year. Mike reaches out to his insurance professional and discovers a supplemental disability plan that is built to protect retirement plans in case of disability. At $1,300 a year, his premium will satisfy his need to protect his plan.

The Power of a Designated Roth Account
If Mike's employer had offered its employees a designated Roth plan as an option for retirement accumulation, then he could have placed his employer-matched funds—or enough to satisfy the annual limit—into the designated Roth account. If this was available to him, then the money he put into his designated Roth plan would not be taxable upon distribution, even though he would be forced to take his RMD.

If the employer-designated Roth account does not offer a program similar to this example, then chances are the plan is directly connected to a program that has a potentially stronger growth opportunity but also has a potential risk of market loss. With a designated Roth account, if the individual withdrew the entire value of the account and the account experienced a market loss, then the loss would be tax deductible. A non-hardship withdrawal provision may allow you to redirect your employer-based funds to a private plan. Consult your team of professionals to examine your employer-based program for a non-hardship provision.

The Bottom Line
When Mike retires, he will have the following incomes and assets:

- Social Security income—taxable based on traditional qualified distributions.
- Qualified employer matched funds—100 percent taxable.
- A Roth IRA—no taxability and can be taken at any time.
- A life insurance policy with cash available when needed based on FIFO method.
- A coordinated non-qualified investment and insurance portfolio utilizing and practicing the Rule of 100.

If Mike had a designated Roth account, then there would be no taxability. He must begin withdrawals at age 70½.

His plan is to accept his Social Security benefit when it is available to him, begin to draw off his qualified employer fund, and then coordinate his Roth IRA accounts, non-qualified investments, and life insurance cash value, keeping him in a low (or possibly a zero) tax bracket. He plans to avoid the need to draw from his qualified plan by utilizing his Roth IRA and investment accounts for large purchases or unexpected emergency expenses.

His future concerns include:

- providing his family with funds to pay estate tax upon his death;
- the consequences of aging: getting frail, forgetfulness, and the need for extended care;
- the fact that he could end up in a nursing home. His funds are vulnerable because his traditional qualified funds must remain in his name and Social Security number if he cannot work them down fast enough.

Mike is a smart guy; he understands that his retirement portfolio has two parts—an investment portion and an insurance portion. He has researched the odds and realizes that based on his plan he needs:

- a life insurance policy that will help satisfy his estate tax concern, as well as provide a place to build cash value as an additional source of obtainable income that can be used in a down market;
- a disability insurance policy with a retirement benefit feature in the event that he gets hurt or experiences a medical condition restricting him from earning an income;
- a long-term care insurance policy to satisfy the consequences of growing old and frail.

These insurance plans will also protect his qualified funds from being consumed by estate tax, medical costs, loss of income, a down market, and long-term care needs while maintaining the continued growth of his retirement plan.

Fast-forward Twenty Years
Mike has been able to contribute to his portfolio, and at age forty-seven, he is twenty years from retiring and is on track to a healthy financial retirement. But he realizes he needs to take his retirement plan one step further. He meets with his team of professionals, and they establish the proper documents to ensure his plans will be secured in the event of premature death or disability; these two issues can devastate the best retirement plan and can be detrimental to families if the proper documents have not been put in place. Mike now has a comprehensive retirement plan consisting of the proper legal, insurance, and financial opportunities. He is in control to minimize his income tax and optimize his income potential during retirement.

Roth Conversions

A Roth conversion is the process of turning a qualified IRA into a Roth IRA. In order to do this, taxes must be paid on the qualified deductible IRA. Making the funds non-qualified allows funds to be accepted into a Roth. Since the funds change from a qualified IRA to a Roth, the 59½ IRS rule does not exist; however, once the funds are in the Roth plan, they must remain there for five years in order to receive the benefits of a Roth plan. Each Roth conversion has its own five-year waiting period before funds can be removed in order to receive the benefits a Roth account offers.

As of 2012, there are no limits to the amount that can be converted, allowing individuals to pay tax and reposition their assets. A Roth conversion allows the individual to position his or her qualified assets in order to protect them. A Roth IRA can easily be taken and repositioned as a non-qualified asset and protected in a cash irrevocable trust.

In the event that an individual's financial position changes (due to retirement or unemployment), his or her tax status may decrease causing less income tax. This would be a great time to take advantage of a Roth conversion.

The obstacle many people have with a Roth conversion is having to pay tax on the funds they are converting into a Roth. An individual converting $1,000,000 into a Roth in 2014 would likely be in the highest tax bracket.

Roth Conversion Strategy If Earned Income Exceeds the Limit

A loophole for high-income earning individuals surfaced with the implementation of Roth conversions. Remember, to participate in a Roth in 2014, the allowable income limit for a married couple filing jointly is $191,000 or less. The perfect time to convert a traditional IRA to a Roth IRA is when your income is below the Roth threshold and tax liability is low. This could be the year of retirement or the following year. The loophole creates an opportunity to convert qualified IRAs to a Roth IRA for individuals and couples generating an income above the allowable limits.

A Roth conversion loophole allows individuals or couples that earn incomes above this level to position funds in a traditional qualified IRA and then convert the traditional IRA into a Roth IRA as often as they like.

For example, Mary and her spouse are ambitious and over-achieving individuals. At age thirty, their combined incomes are above the limit of $191,000. With the help of their CPA and their financial professionals, they decide to:

1. open a qualified IRA with a bank, investment, or insurance company;
2. contribute to the IRA for the entire year, earning a small amount of interest and knowing they are going to pay tax on the funds as well as the interest they earned;
3. convert the qualified IRA to a Roth IRA at the beginning of each year.

There is some risk involved in this process. Your CPA should be navigating the process in order to avoid IRS issues. The IRS may recognize if this process is done too frequently, and they have the authority to institute the step transaction doctrine. This consists of three steps, or tests, to determine if tax abuse has occurred.

1. The **binding commitment test** implies that there is a commitment within the transaction to complete the following steps, such as having to move the funds to a Roth IRA. Since there is no commitment to move the qualified IRA to a Roth IRA, this step does not apply here. Individuals can choose to keep the funds in a qualified position.
2. The **mutual interdependence test** questions and qualifies the interdependence of the transaction. Is the first step relying on the second step to be worthwhile? Since the first step can function without the second step and is not committed to take the second step, it is independent.
3. The **intent test** is focused on the end result of the transaction and its intent. The focus is on whether or not the transactions are subjective to each other. The answer is likely to be yes; however, this loophole

has been exposed by financial and legal experts and is likely used by the individuals that make the rules.

When IRS guidelines change, your tax plan must adjust. In the event that the IRS closes the loophole, individuals could find themselves paying tax on these funds or forced to maintain the funds in a qualified position. The likelihood of this loophole closing is small since the decision makers probably wrote the guidelines with their interest and the interest of high-income earners in mind.

Do the Benefits Outweigh the Risks?

Once the funds are in the Roth IRA, the funds grow tax free and can be taken out tax free, based on the guidelines of qualified plans. The Roth IRA can easily be repositioned into a non-qualified status and placed in a trust, preserving and protecting the funds for future generations. The Roth IRA can be coordinated with other taxable qualified funds, such as Social Security, pension, and 401(k) type plans to balance tax liability and maximize a tax plan.

The penalty, if it is determined to be a step transaction, is 6 percent of all contributions plus interest earned back to the inception of the Roth IRA. And it is likely that the remaining funds after penalties will be forced to convert to a qualified position.

Example of Strategy at Retirement and during Retirement

For example, while working, an individual earned $250,000 annually and accumulated $150,000 ($100,000 for principal and $50,000 interest earned pre-tax) in a qualified IRA. She retires at the end of the year. The following year, the individual anticipates earnings from Social Security of $25,000. Her strategy is as follows:

- She lies low for a year or two, not creating a strong taxable income, living on her Social Security, and withdrawing from non-qualified savings to meet her expenses. The individual estimates her expenses to be $50,000 annually.
- For the next two years, she converts part of her qualified funds to a Roth IRA while her income is low. The funds that are converted are taxed at a controlled tax rate during retirement. With the help of her CPA, she decides to convert $30,000 annually, creating a taxable income of $55,000 and minimizing the taxability of the funds that are being converted.
- The individual will then have $60,000 in a Roth, which must remain there for five years before it can be used.

- Next, the individual draws off her qualified funds as needed, coordinating the qualified withdrawals and minimizing her tax rate according to the income threshold for that year
- After five years, she can then begin to access her Roth IRA and convert the remaining qualified IRA to a Roth, minimizing her tax exposure while capturing the earned interest.

This method is risk free. It is a strategy-based process of coordinating qualified income with non-qualified assets to allow convertibility of a qualified IRA to a Roth IRA.

Employer Sponsored Plans

Notice that the information presented above is based on Roth IRAs that are independent from employer-sponsored retirement plans. Employer-sponsored retirement plans may have triggers within the guidelines of their plans that allow this to take place or allow the individual to remove funds from the employer-sponsored plan. The trigger is generally in the summary plan description, referred to as the "non-hardship withdrawal provision." This allows individuals that are 59½ or older to withdraw qualified funds as a non-hardship rollover. The rollover takes place with the plan administrator's supervision; it must be a trustee-to-trustee rollover, never touching the individual.

There are also triggers in some employer-sponsored plans that allow individuals younger than 59½ to do the same. These triggers are established by the plan administrators.

Disability and Your Retirement

Disability insurance protects you and your family if the wage earner experiences an accident, injury, or illness that prohibits him or her from earning an income.

Many people believe they are never going to be disabled. They do not consider this possibility unless they experience it or see firsthand how it can affect their family. A disability, whether it is physical, mental, or medical, can be devastating to your family's financial health. The stress of having little to no income is overwhelming.

How Disability Affects Your Retirement Plan

In many cases, a disability will not only put your retirement plans on hold but, if not planned for, also reverse them and exhaust your funds. You should prepare for the worst situation and always protect yourself against that possibility.

Many people take out disability policies, even though they believe they will never need it. Not all are so lucky. One day, a man decided to clean the leaves out of the gutters on his house. He fell off the ladder and broke his back. Although his family had a disability plan that covered 65 percent of his income, they still had to dip into their savings and other non-qualified funds. With three teenage children, expenses were at their peak. Disability insurance is based on your income and its replacement. In this circumstance, disability covered everyday living and household expenses. Add the normal amount of medical co-payments and additional services to maintain the house for this family, and any extra income they had went to pay for these things. Even though they had disability insurance, they were in survivor mode. His wife took care of him and maintained the family; it was a full-time job with overtime but without the pay, and her getting a paying job was inconceivable. Moving forward, he and his family were presented with a plan that didn't leave him out in the cold.

Disability insurance for a person's retirement funds was not available several years ago. Now it is!

While disability insurance covers most or all of your income needs, it does not compensate for the normal retirement accumulation that you would experience while working. Many companies offer a retirement benefits rider attached to your disability plan. So, if the person in the example had the opportunity to add a retirement benefits rider to his policy, the policy would have added to his retirement fund while he was disabled. His retirement fund(s) would have continued to accumulate and grow. Without the rider, the man is playing catch-up, reimbursing his funds, working harder to rebuild his plan. If he didn't have a disability plan in place, his retirement funds would have been nearly or completely exhausted. Imagine the stress, disappointment, and disruption the family would have experienced.

For self-employed individuals, other riders offer compensation for loss of revenue and business costs. For instance, consider a self-employed dentist who becomes disabled and has a receptionist, a dental hygienist, and the standard overhead of running a dental office. A rider attached to a disability program can help offset the losses of not having the full revenue of the dental practice and will pay for another dentist to help, allowing the office to remain open and the staff working.

Qualifying for Disability Insurance

Some of the qualifying considerations insurance companies look at when applying for disability insurance are based on where a person lives and his or her occupation, income, hobbies, age, and health.

Location of residence is important because insurance is state specific; all states have different expectations. Also, certain parts of the country are less desirable and present a high risk to insurance companies.

Occupations are critical to disability underwriting. Some occupations are uninsurable due to the nature of the work, as well as location and environment. Individuals that work solely in their homes with little or no physical communication with people may find it difficult to become insured. This may sound like a no-risk occupation; however, the insurance company has no way of publicly verifying a disability.

Income is a key qualifying element and will determine your disability benefit. As your income increases, it is important to revisit your policy and increase the benefit accordingly.

Some hobbies can also be detrimental to your physical well-being and be high risk to the insurance company.

Age and health are strong elements in any insurance policy. The younger you are, the less expensive the premium is likely to be. In general, an individual is most likely to be healthier at a young age as opposed to when he or she grows older.

Although the process of underwriting for disability is similar to underwriting for life insurance, disability insurance is focused on the physical attributes of the body. A person that is obese will have difficulty getting both life and disability insurance. The disability aspect considers the repercussions of obesity: back issues, developing diabetes, and other related problems. If uncontrolled, diabetes can create problems with the back, eyes, feet, heart, and so on. Any of these problems can prevent you from working. Uncontrolled high blood pressure is an issue as well. If untreated and uncontrolled, it can lead to stroke and heart disease, causing you to become disabled. Although more difficult, it is possible to become insured with certain health problems.

Reaching out to an insurance professional that specializes in disability is important.

What to Look for in a Disability Contract

You should be aware of several possible elements in a disability contract: own-occupation versus any-occupation, elimination period and the length of the plan, and exclusions.

Own-occupation and Any-occupation
Own-occupation refers to your capability to perform your own occupation. In the event that you are disabled for any reason and are unable to perform your own occupation, the insurance company will pay the benefit. If you are unable to perform your occupation but can perform another occupation, then the insurance company will continue to pay the benefit, in part or in full. For example, if a CPA is in a car accident and experiences brain damage and can no longer earn income as a CPA, the insurance company pays the benefit. However, if this person is able to function in society and earn an income bagging groceries at the local supermarket, the insurance company is still obligated to pay the benefit in full or in part as the contract stipulates.

Any-occupation works just the opposite. "Any-occupation" means that the insured must be incapable of working any occupation in order to receive disability benefits. If a person becomes disabled for whatever reason and can perform another occupation, then the insurance company may not have to pay the benefit. For example, a CPA is in a car accident and experiences brain damage and can no longer function as a CPA but is able to bag groceries at a supermarket. He is capable of earning an income, and the insurance company does not have to pay.

A fifty-year-old man was a truck driver for a major interstate trucking company. He hurt himself while helping a friend move. Now, he suffers from severe back pain that reaches down into his legs, and he gets frequent migraines. In order to control his pain, the man was on heavy-duty medications that consequently made him drowsy, and he was unable to drive his car. He placed a claim with his disability insurance carrier. Without knowing the difference, the man thought that his policy was an own-occupation. Shortly after placing a claim, he received a letter from the insurance carrier denying the claim; his medical records indicated that he was able to get another job and earn an income. His story is painful; he is in the process of losing his home. He went through his retirement plan and was headed for welfare.

Own-occupation or any-occupation is reflected in the premium. Many plans offer a combination. For example, it is possible to have an own-occupation policy for several years and then change it to an any-occupation policy. There is nothing wrong with either option in a policy as long as you are aware of what you are purchasing. The premium will reflect the plan.

Elimination Periods and Length of Plans

Most disability programs have an elimination period. An elimination period is a waiting term in which the disabled individual pays for services that would be covered by the insurance company. Oftentimes it is considered a deductible. Elimination periods are predominantly found on intermediate or long-term disability policies.

- A short-term plan will cover the insured from day one to a defined number of days (generally 90 or 120 days).
- An intermediate plan will cover the insured for two to five years (according to your choice) and can have an elimination period.
- A long-term plan will cover the insured for a period of years or until the individual passes away, provided that he or she is disabled for life. This plan will generally have an elimination period.

Elimination periods are not generally found on short-term disability plans. Often a short-term disability policy will complement an intermediate or long-term disability policy in order to have coverage during the elimination period. This is why many people will have a short-term and a long-term policy. For example, a short-term policy will cover them from the first day through the 90- or 120-day elimination period, creating coverage beginning the first day of disability.

The length of an elimination period is reflected in the premium. The larger the premium, the smaller the elimination period, and vice versa. It is wise to compare a policy with no elimination period to having two policies, one being a short-term and the other being a long-term policy. Both strategies will satisfy your disability coverage from day one.

Exclusions

There are times when an insurance company finds the need to exclude themselves for insuring a particular portion of the human body. For example, a client who had had surgery on his knee a few years prior applied for disability insurance. Although the operation was successful, the insurance company chose to offer him a policy excluding anything concerning his knee and any other subsequent disability in relation to it. These exclusions are disclosed and must be signed by the insured upon the delivery of the policy.

Private Disability Policies and Group Policies

A group policy is attached to your employment whereas a private policy is not. In the event that you change jobs, the group policy is non-transferable. Often, a group policy is connected to your sick time and vacation time, and if it is work related, then it is attached to your workman's compensation benefit. The premiums are more affordable with a group policy than with a private policy for those reasons. As the premium in a group policy becomes higher, it is more likely to mirror a private policy.

Considering Fixed Index Annuities

This article is designed to guide you through the phases, help you understand your options, and navigate towards a comprehensive decision when considering annuities.

An annuity is an insurance product. Money is placed in the annuity with the insurance company's promise to pay an amount in the future as a lump sum or in intervals over a decided period of time. Annuities are designed to tailor your objective and are structured for retirement and estate planning purposes. There are two basic phases of an annuity: the accumulation phase and the distribution phase.

Types of Annuities

There are four basic types of annuities: immediate, variable, fixed, and fixed-index. All annuities are tax deferred. This article examines fixed and fixed-index annuities.

A fixed annuity is the simplest of all annuities; money goes in and grows at a declared rate and time schedule. As with all deferred annuities, they have a surrender period—a time period where withdrawals are penalized. At the end of the surrender period, the money can continue to grow based on the terms stated in the contract or can be removed without penalty. Immediately, during, or after the surrender period, the funds can be paid out to the annuitant as income on a schedule set by the insurance company. This is called annuitizing. This is a safe, secure financial tool often used in Medicaid and estate planning. You can never lose money in a fixed annuity.

A fixed-index annuity is a fixed annuity with added features that are designed to help the funds grow stronger while protecting them from market risk and losses. Fixed-index annuities offer the choice of placing money in a fixed position as explained above or positioning some or all the funds in an equity index vehicle. Placing funds in an equity index program offers greater growth potential. Funds are placed with the insurance company and invested there, instead of in the market. The insurance company uses the market indexes, such as the S&P 500, as a barometer to measure the rate of interest that is applied to the annuity contract. This method protects money from the potential losses of being in the open market and returns a conservative to moderate rate with the protection of never losing money.

Fixed index annuities are often used as a financial retirement vehicle to meet all expectations, from conservative programs with bonuses (upfront or scheduled guaranteed interest) to programs that offer the full value of the index growth. Here, the major consideration is that there is no market risk giving downside protection. Fixed index plans have caps (maximum potential growth), participation rates (percentage of involvement in the index growth), and spreads (cost or expense). These allow the insurance companies to navigate in good and bad markets.

Fixed index and fixed annuities are insurance programs that remove risk and offer conservative to moderate growth. Ask your annuity professional which type best fits your objective and why. Ask what are the benefits and how will a particular annuity work in your best interest? Why? What are the pros and cons of each program?

Purpose of Insurance and Annuities

Insurance products and programs are about protecting individuals from peril or risk. Why is a fixed annuity an insurance product, and where does it stand in terms of protection? This is how annuities compare to other insurance programs:

- Life insurance protects your family from financial turmoil in the event of death.
- Disability insurance replaces income in the event that you cannot work and ultimately protects your lifestyle and your family's income.
- Long-term care insurance provides income and resources for extended-care services when a person is physically or mentally incapable, protecting his or her income and assets that would be used to pay for these services.
- Fixed annuities are designed to protect and secure retirement assets while providing tax-deferred growth and financial development.

Annuities can protect your income from running out by utilizing the income-stream-for-life approach.

- Fixed annuities can also preserve and protect an estate's monetary assets for future generations while providing tax-deferred growth, safety, and security.

Understand that there are hundreds of types of fixed annuities. They are designed for many different reasons and situations. Generally, it is not difficult to determine which annuity will fit your particular need; however, there are times when this isn't the case, and it may take time to determine which program works for you.

Determine Your Objective for an Annuity

The first order of business when looking at annuities is to determine your purpose for placing money in an annuity. There are many reasons for opening annuities, but yours needs to be the best reason for you.

Ask yourself what are your thoughts as to the current and future function of the annuity. Make a list of the possible functions that you will need the annuity to accomplish, understanding that they may change. One option may be creating an income stream for life that will complement Social Security. Another option could be securing assets from long-term care issues, ultimately preserving them for your heirs to enjoy.

When looking at annuities, it is important to understand thoroughly what your annuity will do for you and when it will do it. There are annuity contracts that are very complicated to understand and others that are very simple. There are hundreds of annuities on the market, and finding the one that best fits your objective is the first step towards purchasing an annuity. This is easily accomplished by consulting with your insurance professional.

Dynamics of Fixed Annuities

Fixed annuities are designed to protect your retirement assets from financial catastrophe. They can also provide security and protect your retirement income by providing an income stream either for the rest of your life or for a defined period of time. A defined period of time is referred to as a "period certain." An income stream for life can be used to supplement your Social Security, pay for long-term care services, or pay for a long-term care insurance policy. An annuity is a safe and secure place to put your retirement funds. Many fixed annuities offer guaranteed interest rates, bonuses, income riders, and downside protection.

How Are Annuities Secured and Protected?

Banks have the Federal Deposit Insurance Corporation (FDIC), which insures your money in a bank for the first $250,000. The FDIC does not protect money placed in an insurance company. So, how are those funds protected?

The state you reside in imposes requirements on insurance companies in order to do business in your state, as well as to ensure the insurance company's financial integrity. Research the ratings, history, and financial integrity of the company you are considering putting your money into.

- Ask for a financial disclosure of the company.
- Is the company well diversified? Research the company on the Internet.
- Is the company battling legal issues or does it have legitimate complaints against it?

Annuities, like all insurance products, are state specific. How does the state that you live in help to protect your annuity? As mentioned, each state has specific requirements that insurance companies must adhere to in order to do business in that state. A quick visit to your state insurance division's website will answer questions you may want to ask, including the following.

- What are the requirements that insurance companies need to adhere to in order to do business in this state, specifically regarding annuities?
- Does the state require insurance companies to back annuity contracts? If yes, how are they required to back annuities?
- Does the state support a minimum deposit in annuities, like the FDIC?
- Is there an insurance cooperative in the state that insurance companies participate in to support annuities?

Security, Safety, Growth, and Protection

Here is a list of many common reasons people get involved with fixed annuities.

- People want their funds to be secure, safe, and protected from the threat of nursing homes.
- They want to protect the vulnerability of their funds from market volatility.
- They want continued tax-deferred growth.

- They want the comfort of knowing that their hard-earned retirement funds are out of harm's way and are with a company that is big, strong, and secure and maintains reserves required by state regulations.
- They want to be able to use their money when and how they want through income streams or lump-sum distributions.
- They don't want to run out of money.

Annuities can satisfy all these concerns.

Addressing the Adverse Reputation of Annuities

Over the past twenty years or so, especially in the 1990s, annuities have earned a bad reputation. I use the word "earned" for a reason: annuities often deserved the negative rating. However, it is no longer as true today. There are still situations in which people are offered an annuity that does not do what they expected or perceived it was going to do for them. However, the insurance industry—including insurance companies, Life Insurance Management Research Association (LIMRA), and individual state commissioner's offices—have cooperatively cleaned up the industry and continue to supervise and monitor insurance companies, insurance products, and insurance agents to minimize concerns.

Meeting financial suitability is a major supervised responsibility placed on the agent in an attempt towards transparency. The agent must prove to the insurance company that the product being offered is suitable for the client and meets the client's goals and expectations. Financial suitability requires full disclosure of income and expenses to determine that the client has sufficient discretionary income. Assets, the way they are held, and their origination are all disclosed. Client objectives, purposes, and immediate and future expectations are fully reviewed and must meet the standards and guidelines that are acceptable to the insurance company. Otherwise, the insurance company will reject the application and funds.

Training is unavoidable; insurance agents are monitored by the individual insurance companies they represent, as well as by LIMRA and the state insurance commissioner's office. Licenses, professional designations, and appointments expire if the agents do not comply with training regulations and requirements.

Insurance companies have made their marketing material reader-friendly and make the information readily available to the client in the application process. They offer product-specific materials, as well as general materials designed to educate prospective clients and help them make informed decisions. Some companies call the applicants and discuss the product and program that they are applying for in order to make sure the client understands all aspects of the plan.

On top of all of that, the industry is protecting the client from misunderstanding and misrepresentation. The individual considering an annuity must read and understand the pros and cons of the program he or she is exploring.

Although many people purchase annuities without the help of their attorney and/or CPA, these professionals hold fiduciary responsibility and can assist you in making these decisions.

Tax Classifications

Annuities are written in terms of qualified and non-qualified. Qualified annuities are funded with money that has not been taxed, like with a 401(k) or a 403(b). Non-qualified funds have been privately accumulated from all types of sources, such as inheritance, life insurance, the sale of property, stocks, bonds, and savings. These funds have already been taxed. However, you are responsible for paying tax on any interest these funds generate because the interest has not been taxed.

The exception in this case is a Roth account. A Roth program accepts non-qualified money and turns it into qualified money by allowing it to grow tax deferred and tax free upon withdrawal. But Roth plans experience all the negative aspects of qualified money, covered in article 1, "What Few Know about Their 401(k) and Other Qualified Retirement Funds," and in chapter 2. With this in mind, the federal government has placed limits on depositing money into a Roth account. Currently, a person who is younger than fifty can contribute $5,500 annually. For those who are fifty and older, the limit is increased to $6,500 annually. Limiting the opportunity for investing in a Roth makes it attractive and enticing.

Qualified and non-qualified money cannot be mixed or blended into one account. If you want to combine the funds, then taxes need to be paid on the qualified money, thus making it non-qualified. Consult your tax advisor before converting qualified funds to non-qualified.

Qualified 59½ IRS Rule

If you withdraw qualified or non-qualified money from a retirement plan prior to age 59½, then the IRS will penalize you 10 percent (unless it fits the exceptions listed below). Since an annuity is considered a retirement program, it must allow your funds to grow tax deferred. The insurance company must report the transaction to the IRS, and you must include the distribution in your taxes. In the event that you fail to pay this penalty by forgetting to file the information, you may open yourself up to an IRS audit. The insurance company is required to notify the IRS when you withdraw money from a qualified retirement fund. The insurance company will also send you a notification at tax time so you can file this form with your taxes. The following are some exceptions to the 59½ IRS rule as found in IRS Code Section 72:

- When the funds are distributed to a beneficiary due to the death of the account holder. However, these funds are treated as an inheritance and are reported to the IRS at tax time.
- When the account holder has become permanently and totally disabled. You can avoid the 10 percent early-withdrawal penalty but not the potential tax on the withdrawal.
- When used to pay medical expenses greater than 7.5 or 10 percent of the person's adjusted gross earnings. Individuals younger than sixty-five fall into the 10 percent category, whereas individuals sixty-five and older fall into the 7.5 percent category. Again, the transaction is reported to the IRS at tax time, and a tax is applied based on IRS guidelines.
- When unemployed for twelve or more weeks. Under this circumstance, an individual can use these funds without penalty to pay health insurance premiums.
- When used for the first-time purchase of a home. A maximum of $10,000 can be used without a penalty.
- When the funds are used to pay for qualified education expenses.

Taxability upon Distributions

All qualified accounts (except for Roth accounts) are 100 percent taxable. Non-qualified funds fall under the last in, first out (LIFO) distribution methods. These are terms that are used when removing funds from an annuity contract.

The principal or premium "first in" is what funds the annuity contract. The contract earns interest after the principal has been established, making the interest the "last in" funds that enter the contract.

When a withdrawal occurs, the interest is distributed first, which is 100 percent taxable. Once all the tax-deferred funds are distributed, the principal is then distributed. Interest earned on the principal is the only taxable portion of the distribution. For example, an individual is taking money out of his annuity. The first three years is taxable because the withdrawal is all interest. He begins to access the principal in the fourth year. The principal is not taxable; however, any interest that the principal earns is taxable and distributed first. Moving forward, interest is paid out first and principal second.

Triggers and Terms Used within a Fixed Index Annuity

The following are terms you should be familiar with when considering a fixed index annuity.

Fixed growth is guaranteed. The rate is declared on the contract anniversary date and will not change until the following anniversary.

Index growth is based on the choice of indexes and crediting methods, such as the S&P 500, and equity growth. Equity growth is calculated using a crediting method, such as the annual or monthly point-to-point and averaging method.

Point-to-point crediting methods, annual or monthly, calculate the equity growth of the index for that period. Annual point-to-point methods take the index value the day that the contract is issued and the value on the anniversary date. The index growth percentage is credited to the contract after caps, participation rates, and spreads are calculated in the equation. With a monthly point-to-point method, the twelve months are added together on the contract's anniversary and applied to the contract after caps, participation rates, and spreads are applied (if applicable). Averaging methods work similarly to the monthly point-to-point, but the twelve months are averaged.

There are other crediting methods offered. Some are standard to the industry, and some are exclusive to the insurance company. Funds can generally be spread among the methods offered by the particular company you are working with.

A **walk-away contract** allows you to receive the initial principal deposit, as well as any applicable bonuses and their interest and growth, as a lump sum at the completion of the surrender period.

A **two-tier contract** is the opposite of a walk-away and is a conditional contract that places limitations and conditions on the funds after the surrender period.

Annuitization moves your funds from the asset to an income. Once funds are annuitized, the action is irreversible. It is the process of taking the money over a period—from five years to twenty years—or taking it as an income stream for life with the option of refund or no refund.

- Refund means that the heirs will receive any funds that are left in the annuity upon the death of the annuitant.
- No refund, generally used with immediate annuities, means that if you die prior to the depletion of the annuity then your beneficiary will not receive the remaining balance.

The no-refund option will pay a larger payout than the refund option. Frequently, the no-refund option can be backed up by placing a life insurance policy on the annuitant.

Downside protection is a guarantee that you will never lose your principal and any growth that has incurred, locking in on the annual anniversary date of the contract. Fixed annuities and fixed index annuities offer downside protection. This is very important!

Bonus Programs, Caps, Participation Rates, Accumulated Value, and Spreads

Bonuses, caps, participation rates, accumulated values, and spreads are terms for the insurance company to manage and navigate through tough times in order to protect your interest and theirs. Annuities are long-term contracts and contain promises.

Many annuity contracts offer bonuses on your money. This means that the insurance company will contribute a percentage of money (interest) on top of your deposit(s) that will grow and belong to you at the end of the contract surrender period. Larger bonuses are placed on contracts that have longer surrender periods. If the annuitant dies prior to the end of the surrender period, then many contracts will offer the entirety or a prorated portion of the bonus. This should not be the sole reason for selecting an annuity; it is, as stated, a bonus—upfront interest.

Questions that you may want to ask regarding bonus programs and how they relate to caps, participation rates, and spreads/margins include the following.

1. **How is the bonus applied to the contract?**
   The bonus can be applied to the accumulated value of the contract on the first day or any time before the end of the surrender period. For example, a ten-year contract could be credited with the bonus upfront or in the fifth year.

2. **Why is it important to know when the bonus becomes part of the accumulated value, and what does that mean?**
   It is important to know this because one insurance company may offer a 20 percent bonus on your contract based on the initial deposit that is applied at the end of the surrender period while anothercompany may offer a 10 percent bonus upon the inception of the contract. Although 20 percent looks better than 10 percent, the 10 percent offer is better because it will generate interest during the surrender period, and the 20 percent offer does not. Bonuses can be applied to the contract in any year as a single bonus or a gradual bonus. Bonus programs also work in conjunction with the participation rate, caps, spread, and costs.

3. **What is a cap, and how is it affected by the bonus?**
   A cap sets the interest limit that can be applied to the contract. It is the maximum interest rate that can be applied to the contract in that year. Caps are established at the discretion of the insurance company

and can also change at the discretion of the insurance company upon the contract anniversary. They are generally locked in each year for the new contract year. Caps and bonuses are coordinated: the larger the bonus, the lower the cap; the smaller the bonus, or no bonus, the larger the cap or lack thereof.

4. **What is the participation rate?**
The participation rate is the percentage at which the contract will participate in the equity of the index that is chosen. It is part of the equation that is used to calculate the interest credited to the contract. If you are looking at equity indexed annuities, then this is a term you will come across. If the contract participation rate is 100 percent of the equity increase and the increase is 10 percent, then the equation will include the entire 10 percent. In the event that the participation rate is 30 percent and the index equity increase is 10 percent, the equation would be credited 3 percent due to the participation rate

5. **What is the accumulation value?**
The accumulation value consists of the principal, bonus, and interest earned. In the event of death before the completion of the surrender period, the accumulated value would be paid to the beneficiary, based on the terms of the contract.

6. **Will the annuity be using a compounding or simple interest rate calculation?**
A simple interest rate is based on the principal deposit that was originally deposited into the contract. For example, $100,000 grows at 10 percent annually. The contract would experience $10,000 of interest earned that year. In the second year, the interest would be based on the same principal of $100,000.

Compounding interest means that the same $100,000 would experience a 10 percent growth in the first year, making the principal balance $110,000. Interest in the second year would be based on the new principal balance of $110,000, and so on each year.

Both types of calculations are found within the industry, and each insurance company determines the type of calculation it wants to offer. Every annuity program has a predetermined interest calculation and should be discussed prior to applying.

7. **How will the bonus affect the spread, and what is the spread in an annuity?**

A spread, also known as a margin, is the percentage that is deducted from the interest earned in an equity-index program. The spread/margin is a built-in charge (a cost that is a percentage of the growth) that is deducted from the interest earned before or after the cap has been applied. The three questions to ask here are:

1. What is the percentage of the spread that the contract is being charged?
2. Will the percentage change on the contract anniversary?
3. What is the specific relationship of the spread to the cap and participation rate in the program under consideration?

It is important for insurance companies to have participation rates, caps, and spreads. This allows them to manage through the market turbulence and volatility and protect and secure the financial safety of the company, as well as your contract with the company.

How Fees, Charges, Participation Rates, Spreads, Caps, and Margins Interact

The insurance company incurs a cost in handling your annuity. The cost is generally built into the contract through the cap, participation rate, and spread. After all, the insurance company needs to make money in order to survive. Unfortunately, caps, spreads, and participation rates are established by the insurance company and are non-negotiable. If the contract has fees and charges, then they are generally disclosed. The disclosed forms are required to be completed and signed, demonstrating transparency.

Some riders, such as an income rider, will have a cost, and the charge is generally referred to as a "basis point." Each basis point represents a 1 percent cost. So, if the rider is offered at 1.5 basis points, then you are being charged 1.5 percent of the accumulated value. Rider costs are separate from spreads or margins.

Surrender Period, Surrender Period Charge, and Penalty-free Withdrawals

A surrender period is the predetermined number of years when a penalty is applied on distributions, excluding RMD and penalty-free withdrawals. This is the period in which you agree to keep your money active with the insurance company. The purpose of the surrender period is to assure the insurance company that you are committed for a set time. Surrender periods provide a comfort for the insurance companies because they know they will have your funds to work with. The longer the surrender period, the better interest rate, bonus, participation rate, cap, and spread that will be offered. Surrender periods are well displayed in the marketing materials, application disclosure, and contract. All annuities, except immediate annuities, have surrender periods. Surrender periods do not exist in immediate annuities since the annuity is paying out a benefit or scheduled to pay it out. This is referred to as annuitization. If an annuity begins paying out (annuitizing) during the surrender period, then the surrender charge is generally eliminated. Elimination occurs because the annuity is captured and annuitized, and it will either stay with the insurance company until it is exhausted or the annuitant dies and the balance is paid to the beneficiaries.

Annuities have surrender periods that can last up to sixteen years depending on the contract. There are times when surrender periods are insignificant, like when the main objective is to utilize an income rider for a lifetime income stream. Surrender periods and charges are not to be feared; however, knowing how they apply to your circumstances is important to understand.

The one charge that is very easy to identify is a surrender charge. Surrender charges occur when you take money out of your annuity while you are in the surrender period. The surrender charges are generally larger during the earlier years and reduce down to zero at the end of the surrender period. Therefore, at the end of the surrender period, you could withdraw money from your annuity without a surrender charge. If you are younger than 59½, then you are subject to the 10 percent IRS penalty, which is separate from the surrender charge. You should always ask to see the surrender charge schedule, and it should be well presented in a signed disclosure.

Fixed and index annuities oftentimes offer an annual 5 percent to 10 percent penalty-free withdrawal. This allows you to access a percentage of your funds without experiencing a surrender charge. It does not exclude you from the IRS 10 percent penalty on qualified funds if you are younger than 59½. RMDs distributed during the surrender period are considered to be part of the penalty-free withdrawal.

Understanding Walk-away Contracts and Conditional Contracts

A walk-away contract signifies that you have no obligation to the insurance company at the completion of the surrender period. Conditional contracts, known as two-tier contracts, have stipulations that need to be satisfied for you to access your funds or stipulate how you can receive funds. Interest rates, participation rates, caps, spreads, and bonuses are subject to the conditions of the contract.

Both walk-away and conditional contracts have a purpose and should be implemented based on your objective. Important questions to ask are:

1. Is the contract a walk-away contract, or does it have conditions during or after the surrender period?

2. What are the conditions of the contract if it is not a walk-away?
3. If it has conditions, can I opt to make it a walk-away later? And if I can, what are the consequences?
4. If it is a conditional contract, how does it benefit me and my estate?

Understanding the Relationship between the Annuity and the Income Rider

Income riders address the biggest concern that retired people are confronted with—even more frightening than death—running out of money. An income rider is an elected attachment to the annuity for the purpose of creating an income stream for life. It is either paid to the annuitant based on the life expectancy table set by the federal government or paid until the death of the annuitant. In most circumstances, it will pay the annuitant until death; however, there are some income riders that will pay based on the expectancy table. When shopping for income riders, it is important to clarify your needs and objective with the agent.

The annuity is the main financial capsule. It houses the principal deposit, bonus, and potential growth based on your selection of growth vehicles.

The income rider is attached and mirrors the annuity providing extra potential, oftentimes in the form of guaranteed growth when creating a guaranteed income stream for life—your actual life, not the life expectation from a life expectancy table. A true income stream for life provides income until you die, whether or not the annuity has money.

The ten target points presented below are used as triggers to help individuals understand the relationship and functional interaction of the annuity and the income rider.

Target Points	Annuity	Income Rider
Downside protection	100%	100%
Tax-deferred growth	Yes	Yes
Bonus (when applicable)	Yes	Most of the time
Surrender period	Yes	No
Required minimum distribution	Yes	Yes
Penalty-free withdrawal	Yes	Yes
Growth	Fixed or indexed	Fixed
Cost	No upfront fees	Varies
Can be annuitized	Yes	No
Payment options	Several	Income stream for life
Death benefit	Annuity value at death	Annuity value at death

Time to Use Your Money

When you decide that it is time to begin using your money, notify the insurance company, and it will give you a choice as to how the annuity can pay out. If you have an income rider, then the rider will be activated. Activating your income rider is not considered annuitizing because annuitizing is a permanent decision and funds are distributed on a schedule over a period of time: five, ten, fifteen, or twenty years. Lifetime-income streams calculate payouts based on the government's life expectancy chart. Some contracts are based on the life expectancy chart, and if you outlive the chart, then payments stop. Other contracts honor the contract until the death of the contract owner, regardless of age. Even if the annuity runs out of money, the payments continue.

Funds that remain in the account once the annuitant has passed away will generally be paid out to the beneficiaries on file. There are instances, especially with immediate annuities, when the remaining funds remain with the insurance company. This method is referred to as a "no refund" option and increases the annuitized payouts but risks that the annuitant may not outlive his or her money. An income stream for life without a refund works well for healthy individuals who are advanced in years. When individuals with this program exhaust their funds, they will continue to receive a monthly benefit greater than if they had elected a benefit with a refund. The annuity payout pays the life insurance premium and returns most of the funds placed in the annuity when the individual passes away.

In the event that you choose an annuity with riders or conditions, the insurance company and your agent will review your options and help direct you to determine the option that best fits your objective. In the event that it is not set up as a walk-away annuity, they will review the stipulations that will best benefit you and your family.

Secure an Agent

This article provides only an overview of annuities and a starting point to work from; it is impossible to cover everything is this short article. Most important, find an agent you can trust that has your best interests in mind. Above all, make your agent explain everything until you feel comfortable with the product and fully understand it, for the product is likely to outlive the agent.

The Role of Life Insurance and Your Retirement Plan

Originally, whole life insurance was the only insurance available. But with the creation of term insurance, followed by universal life insurance, we have options to choose from. With these three types of insurance, we can now make choices that were unimaginable a hundred years ago. These options and changes are beneficial as they help keep the pricing down by creating competition; however, they also make the process of purchasing life insurance complicated. When discussing life insurance as a component of your overall retirement strategy, it is easy to become perplexed. This article will provide clarity, but you still should seek the advice of an insurance professional who can give guidance for your specific situation.

When planning for retirement, life insurance can have several functions—it is a place to accumulate wealth for retirement, it is a tool for planning estate tax, it is a vehicle that can protect your family's lifestyle, and it is capable of passing wealth to beneficiaries.

Term (temporary), universal life (permanent), and whole life (permanent) each has a purpose and works well when applied to the proper need. It is possible to purchase the wrong type of insurance, and it is easy to misuse it.

Term Life Insurance

Term life insurance is generally set for a determined number of years, such as one, ten, fifteen, twenty, twenty-five, or thirty years. As a person grows older and completes the final year of the term, the policy continues to renew on an annual basis; therefore, it is referred to as an annual renewable term (ART). ART is a one-year term contract. At this point, the premium can increase annually and eventually becomes overly expensive and unaffordable. Term life insurance's most attractive attribute is that it is generally less expensive than a permanent policy when purchased at a young age.

Once a person reaches his or her fifties, permanent life insurance becomes generally more affordable. When shopping for term insurance, it is important to closely review the policy illustration and understand how the premium will change at the end of the specific term. If there are asterisks on the policy description page, read and understand their purpose. Ignoring them may be detrimental to your understanding of the policy.

Generally, a term policy will not insure an individual past a certain age. The life expectancy chart provided by the government predicts that most individuals will pass away in their eighties. When reviewing the illustration, it is likely that the premium is extremely expensive and most likely unaffordable prior to reaching this age. If you are looking for a life insurance policy that is going to pay upon the death of an individual no matter the age, then a permanent policy will work best.

Some instances where term is best used are:

- if you cannot afford a permanent policy and need to protect your family for a specific period of time;
- as a mortgage-protection plan that protects your home and its equity while also paying down your loan;
- for insuring short-term business investments and ventures, protecting your family from losses or bad investment decisions in the event of your death;
- in buy-sell agreements for business partners providing the surviving partner with resources to purchase the other partner's share and providing financial resources for the business to move forward;
- to support the co-signing of student loans for parents in the event that their son or daughter dies prematurely so the loans can be satisfied.

Term Convertibility for Individual Plans

Most term policies have a convertibility feature, either for a period of time or for the entire life of the contract. This feature allows the insured to convert a term policy to a permanent policy without medical underwriting. Depending on the contract, policies can be converted based on the individual's contract classification or to a lesser classification, such as preferred to standard.

A private (not group) term policy will convert to a permanent policy whereas a group term policy will convert to a private term policy, not a permanent one.

A conversion feature is beneficial for the individual who has a non-life-threatening medical problem or condition that would place him or her in a ratable category above standard. For example, a person diagnosed with a condition such as diabetes is generally classified as two to three tables above a standard rating, which will create a higher premium. In this situation, the insured can convert his or her term policy to a permanent policy, and the converted rate would reflect a less expensive premium than the premium of a policy with a diabetic rating.

When converting a term policy to a permanent plan, the policy converts at your current age, which in most companies is the age at your nearest birthday. At fifty-four, six months and a day, the person would be considered fifty-five years old.

Fixed vs. Variable Products

Both whole life and universal life plans as discussed below offer fixed and variable programs. The policy structures for both plans generally work the same. The two major differences are that variable products are supervised by the Securities Exchange Commission (SEC) and the state's Department of Insurance and that funds are capable of investing in the open markets. A fixed product falls under insurance regulations and does not participate in the open market.

With a fixed index product, the insurance company is using the equity of the index growth as a measuring device used to calculate interest growth applied to the policyholder's contract.

Premiums paid to an insurance company, placed in a fixed product are contributed to the insurance company's portfolio. The insurance company may be investing in the open markets and responsible for the company's growth or losses with no reflection to your contract. The insurance company could experience a market loss due to bad decisions, but if the index allocated in your contract has grown, the insurance company is obligated to credit your contract regardless.

Universal Life

Universal Life (UL) is considered a permanent life insurance because it can provide coverage until death, provided the policy is structured to do so. It can also act as a term policy; it can be structured to provide coverage for a period of time and lapse. The insurance company agrees to insure you to age 120 or 150, but you decide what age you want to fund it to.

If you fund a UL policy to age eighty-five and find that you need to extend coverage, you can do so by contributing additional money beyond the current premium. If extending the policy becomes necessary, the premium, unlike a term policy, is still based on the age of application since the policy is structured to age 120 or 150.

By increasing the premium, the cash value will increase and will be used to offset the cost of insurance as it increases within the policy, extending the length of coverage. Universal life insurance is an in-between plan since it can work as a term policy and a permanent plan.

Universal life insurance is a cash-value plan offering guarantees that are similar to whole life insurance. A fixed universal life policy can be structured so that the growth responsibility is put on the back of the insurance company, similar to a whole life.

In addition, UL can offer optional growth mechanisms linked to equity indexes or market growth, putting some of the growth risk on the shoulders of the insured. These policies are called equity indexed programs. Although these programs provide downside protection and can never lose money, there is a risk factor: the growth mechanisms, such as the equity index in a fixed program, may not perform as anticipated. On the other hand, the growth may exceed your expectation. However, the policy structure of universal life and whole life offers individuals a guaranteed minimum growth, regardless of the chosen growth mechanism. Both provide the opportunity to accumulate money for retirement and protect the family from loss of income due to death.

With an equity indexed program, the responsibility is also placed on the policyholder and the agent to structure the policy to fit the objectives of the individual, whereas the whole life policy encompasses all of these concerns.

One major concern when structuring a universal life plan is return of account value (referred to as "Option B" or "Option II" in a policy), a feature that can be added to a universal life policy for additional premium. When accumulating for retirement, if you overfund or fund the policy according to the plan, return of account value adds the cash value to the face value, creating a death benefit equal to the face and cash values combined. Without adding this feature to the policy, the face value is paid to the beneficiaries, and the cash value remains with the insurance company upon the death of the individual. Whole life policies address this by offering additional paid-up insurance, increasing the face value as the cash value grows.

Whole Life

Whole life is the oldest form of life insurance and is considered to be a permanent plan. I use "considered" because there are some whole life plans that do not insure the individual until death. For instance, it is possible to be insured under a whole life policy until age seventy-five, which contradicts the implication of the name "whole life." Originally, whole life plans insured the individual until age 100. Today, a whole life policy will insure the individual to age 120; some policies cover to age 150. Check with your insurance company to find out at what age your policy terminates.

Whole life is often thought to be more expensive than universal life. Most whole life plans provide stronger guarantees and accommodations built into the policy that insure against potential structural failure. Universal life does not have these features built in; they need to be added to the base policy and structured into the policy. Fixed whole life policies are focused on a steady guaranteed growth plan. Universal life policies can be structured to do the same but are built to be more flexible in this area.

The opportunity to have different growth opportunities can be good and bad. They are based on the growth of equity indexes, similar to an equity index annuity. A fixed whole life program is not equity-index driven. It boils down to this. With a fixed whole life policy, you know what you are getting with no market risk—only guaranteed growth. With a fixed universal life program, you have a smaller guaranteed growth with the potential of meeting and exceeding the growth of a whole life program, as well as the potential of not meeting the guaranteed growth of whole life. The potential growth of a universal life policy can be left in the hands of the policyholder or of the financial professional.

When comparing whole life and UL among insurance companies, dividends should be addressed. Mutual insurance companies generally offer dividends on top of interest growth with whole life plans whereas insurance companies with stockholders do not. UL programs do not have this advantage.

Life Insurance and Estate Tax

When you die, you are obligated to pay federal and state taxes on your estate if your estate is valued above the federal and state limits. Estate tax must be paid within nine months of your death if you are unmarried or upon the death of the second spouse in a married couple. Federal and state government can change the limits. We are given the tools (LTCI and trusts) to protect your hard work; however, we need to implement them to protect your estate from this tax.

The 2014 and 2015 federal estate tax limit is $5,340,000, and the Massachusetts state limit is $1,000,000. If one's estate is valued above these limits, one will be subject to paying tax on the estate. Hopefully, if it is valued above $1,000,000, you have the proper tools in place to protect your wealth for your heirs. If so, you probably have a whole life or a universal life insurance policy, whether it is an individual or a second-to-die policy in an irrevocable life insurance trust (ILIT). Either one will work for you if properly structured, protected, and geared to your objective. Life insurance, if properly protected in an ILIT in an estate plan, is a tax-free event, and the cash and face values are considered outside the estate when calculating your overall estate value.

Commonly, the overall cost of the insurance policy is less than the death benefit (proceeds) of the policy. For example, at age fifty-four, one takes out a $400,000 universal life policy. The premium is $3,995 annually. If the individual lives a life based on the life expectancy table, then he or she should live another thirty-one years. The total cost will have been $123,845, and his or her family will receive $400,000 tax free. This can be used to pay all or part of the estate tax.

Although whole life insurance can be more expensive than a universal life policy, the premium will stop once the policy is considered paid-up, assuming there is a paid-up feature. A paid-up feature is when the cash value equals the face value. With universal life plans, the premium will continue until death(s) of the insured unless the policy is overfunded to reach 120 or 150 years old.

In order for a universal life policy to be considered paid-up, a single premium can be placed in the policy. A single premium is usually large and will create a modified endowment contract (MEC), which is a change in the policy (insurance contract) when the annual cash contributions in a given year exceed the allowable limit established by the IRS. This will apply a tax on the gain if funds are withdrawn prior to death. However, if there are no withdrawals prior to death, then the benefit is not taxed.

Favorable Tax Benefits for Life Insurance and Income during Retirement

Life insurance can work in coordination with your retirement plan; it may store and develop non-qualified assets to offset a down market and the tax on qualified money. When the market is not returning what you expected and you are depending on the asset growth to provide income, it can be detrimental to pull money from those investments for everyday income. The cash value in a life insurance policy can alleviate the stress from your investments.

By taking money out of your investments in a down market, the principal balance, which creates an income, is drawn down. With a fixed whole life or a fixed indexed universal life insurance policy, your money grows with guarantees. By taking money out of a life insurance policy, your investments are given a chance to recuperate and recapture their losses. Without this in place, you will continue to draw down your investment for income from a program that should be left alone to regenerate.

During a strong and positive market, it is common to pull money from investments. Cash-value life insurance is a stress-reducing way to support the investment portfolio while providing a financial safety net for your spouse in the event of your death. Managing your investment portfolio with your insurance portfolio is important and necessary. Having a life insurance policy with a strong cash value is essential to survive a difficult economy and protect your income, assets, and family from financial devastation.

Since the cash value in a life insurance policy is non-qualified, coordinating cash value withdrawals from a life insurance policy with qualified withdrawals, such as RMD and additional qualified withdrawals, will help balance any tax liability.

Understanding FIFO, LIFO, and the importance of keeping your life insurance contract from becoming a modified endowment contract (MEC) are major tax advantages for retirement.

A MEC is most commonly found when planning for estate tax purposes or when the policy will not have any distributions until the death of the insured.

Coordinating your cash-value life insurance policies is essential in optimizing your retirement opportunities and protecting investment growth, income, and taxability. Cash value, dividends, and earned interest grow tax deferred, and principal distributions are tax free. Staying below the MEC limit when paying a premium is important when using life insurance for retirement purposes.

A life insurance contract becomes a MEC when it fails to meet the seven-pay test. The seven-pay test prevents policies from being paid up prior to the end of seven years. The MEC rules apply to policies written after June 20, 1988.

When the cash value is kept below the MEC level, the first in, first out (FIFO) method of disbursement is used. Since the money coming out of the policy was the first funds (premium) placed into the policy, the funds are tax free. This helps offset the need for taxable income. Once the principal is distributed, the interest is then distributed and taxable.

The 59½ rule applies once a policy becomes a MEC; any individual under the age of 59½ who withdraws from the MEC will be penalized 10 percent by the IRS, and the gains are distributed before the premiums (LIFO method) and are therefore taxable. After the seventh year, the policy must remain below the guideline premium as presented in the contract; otherwise it becomes a MEC.

Many policies automatically adjust the death benefit to accommodate a MEC if designed to do so, or the premium is returned. Policy illustrations will disclose the point when the policy becomes a MEC or meets the guideline premium. Funding up to this point is acceptable, but once a life insurance policy becomes a MEC, it is irreversible.

If the policy becomes a MEC and is paid as a death proceed, the proceed is not taxable. (If the premiums are paid by the individual, the death proceeds are tax free. If the premiums are paid by a corporation, the death benefit is taxable to the individual.) Coordinate with your insurance professional and your tax advisor.

Life Insurance, Qualified Distributions, and Social Security

When withdrawing qualified money from a retirement plan, income tax must be paid on the distribution. By coordinating or limiting qualified income to the required minimum distribution (RMD), income needs above the RMD can be taken out of the cash value of a life insurance policy. If you are planning this as a strategy for retirement, then there are many companies with programs that will fulfill this capacity. Coordinating the cash-value distributions with qualified investments in a healthy market allows you to control your income tax and ultimately protect your Social Security from greater taxability.

Although life insurance is included in the value of an estate, upon death, the beneficiary in most circumstances will experience the death benefit tax free and will be able to continue life without financial trauma.

The insurance policy is being used as a retirement savings vehicle during the accumulation phase. It is important that the plan allows the cash value to join the face value upon death. Permanent policies can be designed to do this for you. As the cash value grows, the face value should grow, taking into consideration the strength of the cash value through additional insurance as with a whole life policy or return of account value as with a UL product. These features are optional and are based on your objective and the design of the policy.

Many of the features will automatically adjust the death value with the increase of cash value, adjusting to the MEC limit in order to avoid a taxable event. As the cash value increases, the death-benefit increases and accommodates the growth proportionately. A life insurance policy must be designed to perform in this manner.

The terms "return of account value," "Option B," and "Option II" are synonymous and will position the cash value with the face value and create a death benefit in a UL program. Option A, the opposite of Option B, allows the cash value to remain with the insurance company upon the death of the insured. The beneficiary receives the face value, not the cash value. Although Option B adds cost to the premium, it adds the cash value to the face value, creating a larger death benefit.

When reviewing the policy with Option B, the cost of insurance generally increases dramatically around age sixty. Consider offsetting Option B with additional face value at the onset of the policy.

How to Recognize Options A and B on a Policy

Option A is referred to as a level death benefit because the payout remains the same, or level, for the life of the insured. The death benefit will not change unless there is another feature, such as additional paid-up insurance, as in a whole life contract. Option B has an increasing death benefit over time because of the accumulation of cash value.

The options are generally displayed at the beginning of the contract on the policy description page with the face value and in the illustration (an insurance term for a text-and-hypothetical graphic presentation of how a policy will perform under specified conditions). Whole life and UL insurance policies present the illustration with the policy presenting the guaranteed, current growth and the optimal growth potential (referred to a non-guaranteed) based on the chosen program.

The following example will give you an idea how Option A can have a negative impact on your life insurance policy and will put Option B into perspective.

A few years ago, I met with a gentleman in his late fifties who presented me with a policy that was issued when he was in his thirties (twenty years ago) in which he had been tucking money away for his retirement. It had a fairly sizable face value and $250,000 in cash value. He had one problem: his money was in Option A. In a nutshell, if he were to die, then the cash value would remain with the insurance company, and his family would receive the face value. The $250,000 that he had worked hard to save would become the insurance company's property.

He was in disbelief. I pointed to the language in the contract and untangled the descriptive web of words comparing Option A to Option B. Although he was under the impression he had Option B, I then showed him his illustration with the face value never changing, proving he had Option A.

The man was shocked and chose to do some research on his own. A week later, I received a call from him requesting another meeting. He had researched his policy and confirmed my findings. What he found distressed him, and he wanted to know how to correct his policy in order to fit his objective.

He had several options:

1. He could move the funds to a different life policy via a 1035 Exchange and maintain the same retirement strategy. However, the cost to do this was a negative factor since the cost of insurance twenty years later would be much greater.
2. He could take a withdrawal and place his funds wherever he chose.
3. He could move the funds to an annuity.

With the assistance of his CPA, they calculated the over-funded portion of his cash value leaving the illustrated value plus the interest that was earned with the policy in order to maintain the policy as intended without tax implications. He decided to place the funds in an annuity. Although using an IRS 1035 Exchange to move his cash value wasn't necessary, it was done anyway to ensure there would be no tax consequences. A 1035 Exchange allows funds to move between insurance products without creating a taxable event. Although the tax method of receiving funds from the annuity is LIFO instead of the FIFO, we were able to rescue his funds in the event of his death.

Reviewing the illustration with your attorney or CPA prior to accepting a policy will help avoid confusion.

Taking Money Out of a Permanent Life Insurance Policy

There are two ways to keep your policy in force when taking money out of a life insurance policy. The first is to take a direct withdrawal, which removes the funds from the policy and reduces the death and cash values. If the policy is designed to use the cash value to fund your retirement, then this is a viable option. By adding additional premium to a UL contract—if structured using "return of" or "increasing" account value (Option B, or II)—the death benefit automatically increases. As withdrawals are made, the death benefit decreases back to its original face value. Managed properly, this method over an extended period of time can be effective and beneficial because it captures a strong interest rate during the accumulation phase without being charged interest at withdrawal. During the distribution phase, it is important not to withdraw more than the additional premium. Exceeding the additional premium through distributions will take money from the original scheduled cash value. If money comes out of the original scheduled cash value, the policy will not have funds to offset the cost of insurance as it increases, and the policy can lapse.

The second way is taking a loan against the cash value. Although taking a loan against your own money sounds counterproductive, it may be a viable and beneficial opportunity.

When taking the loan approach, there are generally two options to choose from. The language in the policy determines your choices. Loan rates are also generally fixed and disclosed in the policy. Older policies may not have the same options that recent policies offer. Before purchasing a life insurance policy, discuss and consider these options.

The first loan option is a wash. This is when the loan amount is taken from the cash value and held separately in its own account. The account with the loan is credited equally to the loan interest, dollar for dollar. The borrowed money is neither contributing to nor drawing from the cash value. The cash value minus the loan continues to grow as allocated, and the death benefit remains the same.

The second loan option is a participating loan, which keeps the loan within the cash value and allows the loan value to contribute to the policy growth. If the policy allocations grow greater than the loan interest, the surplus is added to the policy. For example, John has $200,000 in cash value growing 8 percent annually. He borrows $20,000 at 5 percent from his policy. The loan interest (5 percent) is paid out of the total performance (8 percent). Therefore, the $20,000 loan value continues to work, generating a 3 percent contribution to the cash value. If the cash value grows less than the interest on the loan, the cash value will experience a negative impact.

Both loan options can be changed anytime by the policy owner, and the loan value can be paid back while the insured is alive or settled upon death by a reduced death benefit.

Life Insurance with Long-term Care Riders and Living Benefits Enhancements

Accelerated/living benefit endorsements and long-term care (LTC) riders are enhancements to a life insurance policy that accelerate the death benefit while the individual is alive. The benefit pays out a percentage of the face value that can be used to provide funds, assisting the insured through a health crisis.

An accelerated benefit rider is different from an LTC rider and breaks the benefit down into three categories: terminal, critical, and chronic. This type of program is not underwritten and is not considered a tax-qualified long-term care plan. The plan can be paid out as a lien, which may be taxable, or as a direct advance from the face value and is not taxable.

- A terminal illness benefit is implemented when the insured is diagnosed with a terminal illness and the life expectancy is within the period specified in the policy, usually less than two years.
- Chronic illness benefits are implemented when the insured is incapable of performing two of the six activities of daily living (ADLs): bathing, continence, dressing, eating, toileting, and transferring.
- Critical illness is offered when a person experiences a life-changing illness, such as a stroke, cancer, heart attack, organ transplant, etc.

With most companies, this feature is an election with no added charge to the policy. The election can create a problem with Medicaid planning. This possibility is pointed out by the insurance company on the election/disclosure form.

Each category listed above is treated independently and has individual limits. Once one category's limit has been exhausted, the others are not available until the insured meets the criteria. The insured or his or her representative must apply for the benefit annually, and the funds are distributed as a lump sum. It is not a reimbursement program; therefore, the funds can be used for anything. There is no elimination period, and it doesn't have an inflation mechanism. Premiums are generally paid until death unless a waiver of disability or waiver of premium is in force at the time the claim is filed.

A long-term care rider is a form of an accelerated benefit rider, attached to a life insurance policy. However:

- Federally, a long-term care rider is a tax-qualified plan. Each state differs in tax qualification.
- It is separately underwritten for LTC qualifications.
- It requires additional premium.
- There is an elimination period, generally ninety to one hundred days.
- The policy reimburses expenses spent on the care of the insured, instead of in a lump sum.
- The benefits are comprehensives instead of categorized.
- The entire face value can be used instead of percentages based on category.

If an individual cannot qualify for a long-term care policy, then it is beneficial to consider a life insurance policy with an enhancement program. The best program is usually a standalone LTC policy because it is comprehensive and independent. A combination life insurance policy with a long-term care rider is an in-between plan that is designed to satisfy long-term care needs utilizing the face value.

Enhancements, such as a living benefit rider, can affect the qualification process for Medicaid. Insurance companies have emphasized this concern, and it is clearly stated on the election form. This is another reason why it is important to have a team of experts focused on your objectives, each working independently in his or her field of expertise.

Conclusion

There are three life insurance programs offered in today's market: term, universal, and whole life. The end results of the insurance policy you set up are determined by how it is structured, based on your objectives. Life insurance can be a great element for retirement when designed and structured properly. The recommended team approach to organizing your estate is essential to meet and optimize your objectives.

Life insurance can play ten important roles during retirement and afterward.

1. Life insurance acts as a safe, secure vehicle to accumulate non-qualified funds, which can be used to counteract taxation on qualified funds. Coordinating and controlling qualified and non-qualified funds and minimizing taxability are objectives when retired.
2. Life insurance can provide income during a down market, allowing investments to regenerate and help preserve the principal.
3. In a down market, life insurance takes the burden off your investment portfolio and protects your family from experiencing greater market risk or financial strain caused by unexpected death while also protecting income.
4. Life insurance provides your estate and family with the funds to contribute and satisfy estate tax.
5. Life insurance contributes to the family's income by protecting assets and can replace the income you contributed to the family's daily living. Without this, they may have to liquidate and adjust their lifestyles to meet their obligations.
6. Life insurance offers living benefits to provide financial resources during critical, chronic, and terminal illness if a long-term care policy is not in place. This will help protect assets and household income from devastation.
7. Life insurance provides the insured with a sense of relief knowing he or she has done everything possible to provide for the family by keeping them from financial devastation due to death or illness.
8. Financially, life insurance protects and preserves what you have worked hard to accumulate and accomplish.
9. Life insurance sends a message to your family that you care.
10. Life insurance can be the biggest gift you ever give to your family.

ARTICLE 7

Understanding the Irrevocable IRS Qualified Retirement Trust

In order to understand the irrevocable IRS qualified retirement trust, we must first define and discuss the values of a revocable trust, an irrevocable trust, and a qualified terminable interest property trust and how they relate to an irrevocable IRS retirement trust.

A trust is a private legal document that presents a person's wishes before and after death. (A trust differs from a will, which is a public document, filed at the probate court in the county in which the individual resided. When probating a will, the personal representative must file an inventory of assets that were in the deceased's name only.) Trusts avoid the expensive process of probating an estate.

A revocable trust holds countable funds used for everyday living, such as a checking and savings accounts, as well as life insurance and investment accounts that may be used during your lifetime. A revocable trust is taxed via the individual's Social Security number and remains within the individual's estate. The disposition of assets can be changed at will. Since the funds are countable until death, there is no look-back period and, therefore, cannot be protected from long-term care expenses.

An irrevocable trust has a separate federal identification number and is taxed independently. The funds within the irrevocable trust are considered protected from estate tax and long-term care expenses once it is past the look-back period. The look-back period is currently three years for estate tax purposes and five years for Medicaid purposes. The substantive terms of an irrevocable trust cannot be changed; however, the donor (also called a grantor or settlor, the individual establishing the trust) can add, remove, or replace a trustee according to the terms of the trust. The donor relinquishes all other responsibilities over the trust to the trustee, who must follow the terms of the trust that you have established. The trustee is responsible for yearly accounting to the beneficiaries and filing a trust tax return. The trustee can be a family member, friend, or a third-party representative, such as an attorney or CPA.

The requirements for a trust to qualify as a designated beneficiary are the following.

- The trust must be a valid trust under state law.
- The trust must be irrevocable at death.
- The beneficiaries of the trust must be identifiable.
- A copy of the trust document must be provided to the plan by October 31 of the year following the year of the IRA owner's death.
- The beneficiaries of the trust must be individuals.
- No person may have the power to change the beneficiaries after December 31 of the year after the participant's death.

If these requirements are met, then the trust qualifies as a designated beneficiary, and the trust beneficiary's life expectancy can be used to calculate post-death required minimum distributions. If the trust fails to qualify, then there is no designated beneficiary and trust beneficiaries will not be able to stretch post-death required distributions over their life expectancies. In that case, the IRA will be paid out either under the five-year rule (if the IRA owner dies before his required beginning date, or RBD) or over the remaining life expectancy of the deceased IRA owner (if the IRA owner dies after his RBD).

Understanding the Role of a Qualified Terminable Property Trust before Initiating a Retirement Trust

A qualified terminable interest property (QTIP) trust may be revocable or irrevocable and is established when the donor wishes to provide for his or her spouse, family member, or friend while protecting the descendant's inheritance. The funds placed in the QTIP trust can be qualified or non-qualified. A QTIP trust can be funded prior to or after death. Once an irrevocable trust is established, the trustee is in control and administers the trust according to the donor's intent.

QTIP trusts are designed for many purposes. They are often seen in the estate planning of blended families or individuals that have a need to protect or limit assets after their death for personal reasons, such as a spendthrift spouse or for estate tax planning. An IRS qualified retirement trust can be a QTIP trust.

The IRS qualified retirement trust is a complex document and is used for many purposes, too many to cover in this article. Among the benefits to be considered are:

- $5,340,000 federal unified exemption;
- state-specific unified exemption;
- the trust and not the spouse as the designated beneficiary;
- special privileges for the surviving spouse's income;
- possibly more favorable tax considerations when calculating RMD for the surviving spouse;
- trust is not included in the spouse's estate;
- protects the heirs from a spendthrift spouse.

Until the donor's death, the donor must receive RMDs if the funds are qualified and may take additional distributions as desired. The trust can be designed to provide for the needs of a spouse. The trust may be designed to eliminate a spousal rollover since the trust has its own identity. The IRS qualified retirement trust offers tax advantages for the spouse since it may not be rolled over as an inherited IRA or can be limited in value to the spouse. The trust dictates the age and amount of the distributions the descendants receive, such as when the heirs are in a lower tax rate. An IRS qualified retirement trust may fund your children's trust or a grandchild's trust. The funds in the trust, for the benefit of the child and grandchild, may be protected from creditors.

Irrevocable IRS Qualified Retirement Trust for a Blended Family

One popular purpose of an irrevocable IRS qualified retirement trust is in a blended family. For example, John and Sue are in their sixties, have been married for thirty-five years, and have three children. Both John and Sue have accumulated substantial wealth by generously contributing to their 401(k)s. Sue passes, and John inherits her 401(k). John now has a very large qualified retirement fund.

Five years later, John meets Jane, and they decide to marry. She has three children from her previous marriage. Jane was a stay-at-home mother and never worked. Her late husband left her a 401(k) as well, but nothing near the value of John's. Soon into the marriage, John realizes that Jane loves to spend money. She agrees and is concerned that without John she would run out of money.

John's concern is that if he predeceases her, Jane will spend all his retirement funds or may need it for long-term care since she does not have long-term care insurance. He also feels that since his retirement funds were combined with his late wife's funds, he would like the principal balance upon his death to be left to his children once Jane dies. He wants Jane to receive the interest earned from his funds while she is alive, as well as the assets they have accumulated during their life together. Based on their assets, the interest earned should be sufficient; however, he wants to allow the trustee to determine her need at that time.

John and Jane openly discuss their concerns with their estate planning attorney. John's three children have also recognized and voiced their concerns. Jane's three children are excited that she married John since the gifts they receive have become more frequent and of better quality. Since John is concerned that there might be some animosity from his children as to the placement of the asset, he has appointed his attorney as his trustee.

If John predeceases Jane, John's qualified funds will be placed in an irrevocable trust with its own tax identification number. Their attorney will become the trustee and will oversee the funds, accounting, and tax reporting, as well as distributing the interest to Jane. If Jane needs long-term care and the trust is beyond the look-back period, Jane will apply to Medicaid if she needs to enter a skilled nursing facility. If she receives home health care, she has access to the funds through the discretion of the attorney. When Jane passes away, John's qualified funds will be distributed to his three children according to the terms in the trust.

IRS Qualified Retirement Trust for a Spouse with No Need for the Funds

Another popular use for an IRS qualified retirement trust is when an estate has substantial assets and the spouse has no need for the qualified asset. In this event, upon the death of the donor, qualified funds can be placed in a child's trust and/or grandchild's trust. Interest can grow within the trust and/or be distributed to the child according to the trust. The trust can be designed to have all or part of the funds skip over the spouse directly to the child's and/or grandchild's trust. In the event the spouse is in need of long-term care in a skilled nursing facility, this would protect the funds from being used and could assist in qualifying for Medicaid. In this example, if the spouse had a long-term care insurance policy, the interest from the funds in the trust can be assigned to pay the premium for the policy if the terms of the trust allow. If the funds are large, the interest can be released to pay for long-term care expenses, again provided the trust allows for such action.

Children's and Grandchildren's Trusts

Income received by the children and grandchildren from the trust is taxed at their individual rate with the potential of kiddie tax (see IRS tax topic 553). A child's and grandchild's trust allows qualified funds to be distributed, regardless of age, based on the terms of the trust, eliminating the 59½ IRS penalty. Imagine funding your grandchildren's college education with your retirement funds. They, at age eighteen to twenty-four, if filing income tax as individuals, would experience a lower tax rate than when they are generating a personal income.

Conclusion

The previous examples are among many common uses for an IRS qualified retirement trust. An IRS qualified retirement trust is very complex, yet a valuable tool when planning your estate.

In respect to long-term care expenses, the IRS qualified retirement trust will not protect funds from being used on behalf of the donor. The only vehicle that will do that is a long-term care insurance policy. The IRS qualified retirement trust can be designed to protect the funds from being used toward a spouse's long-term care expenses or contribute a controlled amount. In this situation, if the owner of the qualified funds has long-term care insurance and the spouse is uninsurable, a long-term care policy can be placed on the owner, and the RMDs can contribute to the premium through the trust. Upon the death of the owner, the funds would be distributed to a specially designed trust that protects the assets for the descendants with the benefit of helping the spouse qualify for Medicaid sooner rather than later.

If the situation were reversed and the owner of the qualified funds is uninsurable and does not have long-term care insurance, the funds may need to be used for long-term care. Upon the owner's death, the funds could be directed to a trust to fund a long-term care policy for the spouse or self-insure the spouse's care, whichever is beneficial and follows the wishes of the donor.

When the qualified asset is not needed, sending it to the next generation or beyond may be a great alternative, and an irrevocable IRS retirement trust may be the perfect vehicle.

The Role of Long-term Care Insurance and Your Retirement Plan

The simplest definition of long-term care insurance (LTCI) is a type of disability insurance that is used when you cannot function without help. Everyday activities, such as bathing, dressing, eating, toileting, transferring, and continence problems, become impossible without assistance. The need for long-term care (LTC) can be caused by accidents, illnesses, disease, or aging.

Many people don't understand long-term care insurance, how it works, what it does, or why they may need it. Oftentimes, an individual becomes familiar with this process when he or she becomes a caregiver. People usually purchase LTCI policies due to a personal experience or from the recommendation of a professional.

Whether in a skilled nursing facility (nursing home), an assisted living facility, or at home, the emotional, physical, and financial process of aging can be so grueling, harsh, expensive, and invasive that the individual in need of help may consider dying as an easier alternative. With a long-term care insurance policy, uneasy feelings are alleviated because the individual has care specific to his or her needs; there is a level of privacy, and the word "dignity" is redefined.

The LTCI company provides your family with income to pay for the services you need, as well as physical and emotional resources. A Long Term Care Insurance Plan helps take the burden off your family and assists them with the consequences affiliated with long-term care disabilities. It also gives the caretaker peace of mind knowing that he or she has done everything possible to provide the family with the tools that they may need during this time.

There are two reasons why one purchases LTCI:

1. To help the family confront the needs of the individual. This may be with physical and emotional resources, income, and/or support to deal with the consequences of disability and the need for care.
2. To protect income and assets that one's family depends on to support themselves. LTC costs may quickly absorb everyday income and consume assets prior to Medicaid assistance.

There are three reasons why one would not choose to purchase LTCI:

1. Some individuals may not physically, emotionally, or medically qualify for LTCI.
2. Their assets do not need protection. Either they have few assets or the assets have been sheltered.
3. If the individual's assets are strong enough to provide for these services out of pocket, then he or she is self-insuring.

Qualifying for LTCI

The underwriting of LTCI is different from underwriting for any other insurance, accounting for one reason why people don't understand the product. LTCI underwriting is qualified based on the individual's ability to function in normal activities of daily living. Activities of daily living (ADL) are defined by the National Association of Insurance Commissioners as "everyday functions and activities individuals usually do without help. ADL functions include bathing, continence, dressing, eating, toileting, and transferring. Many policies use the inability to do a certain number of ADLs (such as two to six) to decide when to pay benefits."

Health issues and family history, as well as medication and personal medical information, play into the underwriting process.

Cancer is a disease many people fear causes them to be ineligible for LTCI. Luckily, this is not true. Although cancer can be debilitating, it generally has a more defined ending, and ADLs are often functional until the very end. Understanding this shines a light on why hypertension (high blood pressure) is a great concern to the insurance company. High blood pressure, although insurable if under control, can be a greater concern to an insurance company than cancer is when underwriting LTCI. Let's take into consideration a person with uncontrolled hypertension:

- Uncontrolled hypertension can lead to heart attack and stroke.
- A stroke can lead to the person's inability to walk, dress, and bathe, among other ADLs, for an extended period of time.

Since stroke victims have a greater chance of living for an unpredictable period of time, it is a greater insurable risk for the insurance company. The underwriting is based on the ADLs, and stroke victims are able to live longer after having a stroke without the function of their ADLs.

Before you disqualify yourself, call a qualified insurance agent who specializes in LTCI and complete a questionnaire over the telephone. If a traditional program doesn't work for you, there are many hybrid products designed to fit different situations. The agent can discuss your case with an underwriter to determine which programs will work for you.

How LTCI Works

A fifty-four-year-old man fell off his ladder one weekend while he was cleaning the gutters on his home. He broke his back and was laid up in the hospital for three weeks. He was married with three children. He spent three months in a rehabilitation facility and then was sent home to continue to receive in-home therapy for several months until he fully recovered. His employer-sponsored disability insurance paid him, compensating for the man's loss of income to support his family. Fortunately, his health insurance covered the medical and hospital bills.

The man needed help bathing and dressing, so LTCI paid for him to have a professional caregiver assist him with these functions. Without LTCI, the family would have been forced to pay someone to help him and would have dipped into their savings and investments, causing a financial and emotional strain.

If the man in the example had been older, collecting Social Security, and on Medicare, then his situation would have been different. Social Security provides income that was provided by the disability insurance. Medicare replaces his employer-sponsored health insurance paying 100 percent for the first twenty-one days in a skilled nursing/rehabilitation facility and a portion of the cost (generally 100 percent minus a co-pay) from day twenty-two to one hundred in a skilled nursing/rehabilitation facility. After completing one hundred days, the injured man would need to rely on his assets to provide the services needed to bathe and dress on a daily basis. In 2013, the cost of in-home care was approximately twenty dollars per hour. For someone to come in and help the man bathe and dress in the morning and evening would cost around forty dollars a day, or $1,200 a month. LTCI satisfies this expense.

Once I Qualify, What Services Can My Family Expect?

LTCI can provide you and your family with services based on a choice between separate and comprehensive policies. Separate, independent service contracts will provide specific services and may or may not provide a care coordinator. A comprehensive plan will provide all the services listed below, based on the parameters of the contract:

- **Care Coordinator** – Based on the contract, a care coordinator is available, either by phone or in person, to help administer the contract and coordinate services and resources. This person is familiar with your situation and knows the obstacles you face and how to overcome them. This service is not a cost to the contract.
- **Nursing Home Care** – LTCI pays for this service once the elimination period is satisfied.
- **Assisted Living Facility** – This type of community is for individuals in need of medical and personal supervision.
- **Home Health Aide** – Services by home health aides are not medically related, such as cooking, cleaning, shopping, laundry, etc.
- **In-home Personal Care** – This provides services for hygiene and necessities for survival, such as bathing, dressing, grooming, cooking, eating, moving around, etc.
- **Respite Care** – This provides someone to spend time with the caretaker while the caregiver is away or in need of personal time.
- **Hospice Care** – This is provided with LTCI and Medicare during the final days or weeks helping to minimize pain and suffering.
- **Adult Daycare** – This offers activities and social opportunities allowing the individual to continue to be a part of the community.

Many of these services are also offered through the Visiting Nurse Association (VNA), Medicare, the VA, and other local veteran and social organizations; however, these programs are very limited and require the individual to qualify financially.

Medicare and Medicaid are beginning to offer programs such as PACE (Programs for All-inclusive Care for the Elderly), which is an adult daycare program with a team of medical professionals. PACE is a versatile program financially designed for everyone. Medicare and Medicaid will support the cost entirely or with a co-pay for those that meet the financial criteria set by the state they live in. LTCI works well with PACE because it can satisfy the co-pay and will help to extend the value of the LTCI policy providing more services for a longer period of time. An LTCI policy is not meant to eliminate the use of these programs—it should complement them. These programs can help preserve the benefit of an LTCI policy if your benefit has limits. Coordinating benefits between a private LTCI policy and public programs is a great option for a caregiver. LTCI allows you to be in control and provides assisted living and nursing home care, which none of the plans offer coverage for, as they are the two most intense and expensive services.

Reimbursement, Indemnity, and Cash Benefit

Long-term care policies are usually reimbursement programs. In most situations, individuals receive benefits through the reimbursement of expenses. Once a claim is opened, the insurance company follows the claim through the elimination period, which is similar to a deductible. In a home health care environment, once the elimination period is satisfied, expenses based on the benefit terms are paid by the claimant, and then receipts are submitted to the insurance company for reimbursement. Oftentimes in an assisted living or a skilled nursing environment, a relationship is built between the facility and the insurance company; reimbursement will take place without the help of the claimant.

There are companies that offer options such as indemnity (the full daily/monthly benefit is paid out, regardless of expenses) as a selection upon application. Some policies have other options built into the policy, such as indemnity and cash benefits (the option to take partial to full daily/monthly benefit in cash instead of expenses). Oftentimes, these options can be stopped and started according to need. These types of options are helpful when a policy is being used for home health care. The language of the policy will determine these options.

Positive and Negative Impacts of LTCI

Only 14 percent of individuals over sixty years old have an LTCI policy as reported by the Employee Benefit Research Institute, June 2012 Issue Brief. Most people feel that LTCI policies are too expensive until they realize the positive impact a policy can have on their lives at retirement. Let's examine the positive and negative impacts:

Positive Impacts of Having LTCI

- Financially, LTCI protects your family's income and assets, including real estate and qualified and non-qualified funds.
- A single shared plan can protect two people on the same policy. Shared plans cost less than two individual plans.
- LTCI provides your family with the tools and resources to care for you and your spouse or partner.
- LTCI relieves your family of the burden of wondering how they will provide for you and your spouse or partner.

- LTCI gives you the peace of mind that your family's financial stability will not be jeopardized after your death.
- Having a policy eliminates helplessness and despair that may develop in the event that you need care.
- You may never need to use your policy. If you have a combination policy (life insurance with an LTC rider), then it will pay out the remaining interest as a death benefit.

Negative Impact of Not Having LTCI

- Your family has few references and resources for services. Families are left to find them on their own.
- Your family will be forced to spend down or sell your assets, converting assets to cash, which is spent on your care until Medicaid steps in. Families are left with limited assets.
- Your income (Social Security and pensions) will be redirected and used to pay for your care instead of your family's needs.
- An unnecessary strain or burden is put on family members and relationships.

Additional Concerns When a Person Has an LTCI Policy

- The premium is paid from cash flow or assets. Paying for the policy could put a strain on household income.
- LTCI must be paid for, whether it is used or not.

If you are trying to protect less than $120,000, LTCI may not be for you. If you are trying to protect more than $120,000, you should read on. There are different types of plans fit for each situation.

Costs for LTC

Let's address the cost with the following analysis. In 2013, the average cost (nationally) for a room in a semi-private nursing home for one person was approximately $81,000 per year. The national average rate increases 4.1 percent annually.

Let's assume the policy is designed for a couple in their mid-fifties. The premium will be approximately $7,000 annually.

If they were to use their benefit in their mid-eighties—thirty years after purchasing the policy—they would have invested $210,000. The approximate cost of nursing home services thirty years from now will be at least $242,291 per year and continuously increasing. Is $210,000 worth protecting your assets and providing you and your family with the services needed to get you and your spouse through this period of life? If the individual remained in a skilled nursing home for two years, then the cost of care would be $484,582, and the policy would have cost the couple only $210,000, saving them $274,584.

Whether the couple has children willing to care for them strengthens the level of care. Instead of having their children in a hands-on mode, they are in an administrative mode, coordinating and emotionally caring for the individual. The policy is also providing income, protecting the interruption of the income stream going to the spouse.

Typical Situation

The following example uses a couple to present the concept of a shared plan, which is generally greater in cost than one individual plan but less expensive than having two separate plans. A shared plan offers two individuals the opportunity to share the benefit of one policy. For example, if one insured uses 40 percent of the benefit, the remaining 60 percent is left for the other insured.

Let's look at John and Mary Smith's situation:

- John and Mary have been together for thirty years and are in their early fifties.
- They have three children, who they put through college.
- Both enjoy their careers and have been fairly successful.
- Their combined income is $225,000.
- They have a home that they live in nine months out of the year with a small mortgage. They own a summer home with no mortgage.
- As much money as possible was put in their 401(k). They have $700,000 combined.
- They also have some investments that John likes to manage, totaling $300,000.
- Their term insurance will come to the end of its term in five years.
- They both drive leased cars and pay $600 a month combined.
- Their car insurance costs $2,500 a year, and they have great driving records.
- They pay $2,500 a year for homeowner's insurance for two homes.
- Other than a will, they have no legal estate planning documents.
- They have no LTCI, and it will cost $7,000 a year for a comprehensive plan for life, keeping in line with current long-term care costs.

John and Mary are beginning to look at retirement and want to maximize and optimize in all areas, preserving for their children and allowing themselves to enjoy their retirement. They feel that with the help of their children they will be able to stay in their home until the very end. They can't understand why they should take out an LTCI policy (preferably a shared plan, which would be $9,000 a year versus $10,500 for two individual LTCI policies). These are the reasons:

- They each have $350,000 ($700,000 total) in qualified (401(k)) money, which cannot be protected; the income tax on it would be a financial burden. In the event that one of them is placed in a skilled nursing facility, their qualified funds are combined and must be spent down to the state's community spouse limit before Medicaid steps in.
- They have $300,000 in investments with plans to use during retirement. This money is unprotected and vulnerable.
- They have two homes that have not been placed into a trust and are valued at over $1,000,000. Some states have home value/equity limits. Equity levels above these limits are vulnerable unless protected.

In the event that either of them is in a car accident, experiences a stroke, or falls off a ladder and has to be institutionalized, their assets are at risk.

If they fail to put LTCI on themselves but legally protect their homes through estate planning and are beyond the look-back period to qualify for Medicaid, they still have $1,000,000 at risk in qualified funds and non-qualified assets. The expense of an LTCI policy is justifiable, based on their assets and objectives. A shared plan will cover both of them. Individually, the plans would have cost $10,500 annually.

A shared care plan would work well in this situation since it is designed to care for two people. When the first insured needs help, the healthier will be there to assist, along with the children, therefore using less benefit. When the second insured needs assistance, the children will be there, but they may need further assistance, which will create greater and more expenses. If either one needs to enter an extended-care facility and consumes the majority of the policy, the second insured has less. Some polices set limits on the shared benefit protecting some of the benefit for the second insured. No matter how you look at it, the shared plan offers a substantial opportunity to protect a sizable portion, if not all, of their assets for their heirs.

Still, John and Mary were disappointed when it was suggested they redirect a portion of the $30,000 they had been paying for college tuition into insurance planning for their estate. I pointed out that they enjoy driving nice cars and are paying for insurance to protect those assets but uncertain whether they should pay for LTCI to protect the lifestyle they are accustomed to for their children and grandchildren to come.

Very often people who are willing to enjoy life with all its amenities are unwilling to protect what they have worked so hard to accumulate. In

John and Mary's situation, they would have been devastated if something had happened without LTCI protection and could have lost everything.

Fitting an LTCI Policy to Your Needs

Not everyone can afford an LTCI policy. First, determine your financial need.

- The premium must be affordable and should be designed with that in mind.
- Do you have assets that need to be protected?
- If your only asset is your home and it is valued above the state-mandated value, then there are two ways to protect it:
    1. Draw up legal documents, such as a trust, established to reach beyond the look-back period if you plan to apply for Medicaid.
    2. Establish an LTCI policy to meet the minimum need of your state.

In 2014, the community spouse was allowed to retain $117,240 in countable assets plus the resident allowance of $2,000. Adding a qualified retirement plan valued over $119,240 ($117,240 + $2,000) to the assets creates a stronger need for LTCI. So, if you have a house in a trust, are beyond the look-back period, and have around $119,240 in assets, then you may slip through.

Once your spouse dies, the allowable asset level drops to $2,000 before Medicaid will offer assistance. Since it is qualified money, you cannot protect it in the trust; it is accessible and must be used before Medicaid steps in. If you have a house in a trust, are beyond the look-back period, and have over $2,000 in qualified assets, then these assets need to be spent down until the level meets Medicaid requirements. An LTCI policy becomes a needed program in your overall estate plan if you want to save your qualified assets.

If your home is not protected in a trust and you don't have an LTCI policy to cover your assets, then federal guidelines allow Medicaid to take into consideration the equity in your home above $802,000 in 2014 before offering Medicaid benefits.

The second step in fitting a policy is determining what type of LTCI plan fits your needs and qualifications. It is best to meet with a qualified LTC expert because there are many options and types of programs. An expert will help determine which program fits best.

1. **Standalone, comprehensive policies** are the strongest plans and are directed solely toward LTC. They provide services for all areas of LTC needs, making them comprehensive. Inflation protection can be added to the policy.

2. **Standalone policies that are not comprehensive** cover only certain aspects of LTC, such as a nursing-home-only policy or a home-health-care-only policy. These are separate policies and are specifically focused on particular services, which tend to be less expensive than a comprehensive policy.

3. **Combination life insurance and LTCI** riders are very attractive plans because life insurance pays a death benefit based on the money that is left after LTC is paid for.

4. **Life insurance policies with living benefit endorsements** offer terminal, critical, and chronic illness riders. Usually there is no additional cost for these benefits. It is a good alternative for someone who cannot physically, emotionally, or medically qualify for LTCI but qualifies for life insurance. The riders are initially applied for during the application process and implemented when it appears that a person has only a few months to two years to live, depending on the terms of the policy. The three riders are implemented independent of each other and can be exhausted prior to qualifying for another rider.

Qualifying to receive the riders is based on ADL performance and/ or physician prognosis. The insured generally reapplies for the benefits annually. There are limits and guidelines set by the insurance company restricting the amount of money that can be released for each category. The guidelines generally retain a percentage of value to be distributed upon death. There isn't a cost of living adjustment on living benefit endorsements. The program can create a loan against the value of the policy, and the entire loan value is paid back at the death of the individual, reducing the death benefit of the policy. This is called the lien approach, which can be taxable. The opposite of the lien approach is a direct advance, which is not taxable since the face value is released prior to death. Like all life insurance plans, the death benefit is tax free upon the death of the insured, provided the policy is not owned and the premiums are not paid for by a corporation.

LTCI Riders Differ from Living Benefit Endorsements

An LTCI rider is a form of a living benefit endorsement with additional premium. Most LTC riders allow 100 percent of the face value to be used for LTC purposes. This type of plan works similar to a comprehensive standalone plan. It is separately underwritten and has an elimination period; however, it does not typically keep up with inflation (which should be taken into consideration when designing your insurance portfolio) and does not typically have a waiver of premium beyond age sixty-five.

A person who has a $300,000 life insurance policy with a tax qualified LTC rider attached can expect to use $100,000 of the LTC rider for long-term care, and upon death, beneficiaries would have the remaining $200,000 available as a tax-free death benefit.

Hybrids

Annuities and life insurance products are being introduced to assist individuals with alternate ways of providing LTC benefits. These products are built for LTC functions utilizing life insurance or annuities. These programs will multiply the values two to three times for LTC purposes. The funds are generally based on a single premium and have conservative growth with no market risk. The health underwriting is minimal. The funds used for LTC purposes are tax qualified.

Self-insuring Your LTC Needs

For individuals or couples who have accumulated significant wealth, protection is critical. Although LTCI policies are considered self-insuring, there are times when wealth can make LTCI unnecessary. Individuals that can place a large amount of money into a financial vehicle that will guarantee a rate of return large enough to support their LTC needs do not need LTCI.

Utilizing wealth and establishing a pool of money is an alternative way of paying for LTC. There are programs that use income-stream-for-life and nursing-home-confinement riders to meet LTC objectives. Careful analysis will present the best alternative:

- If placed in the proper annuity, then the annuity will never lose money and can grow at a consistent rate.
- If the annuity is never used, then the funds follow the wishes of the owner—generally in a trust.
- If the annuity is using an income-stream-for-life program, then the benefit will last until the insured passes away.
- If the annuitant passes away prior to the depletion of the annuity, then the beneficiary receives the remaining value.

The value of the annuity needs to be compared to the cost and risk factors of LTCI. Some states allow LTC insurance companies to offer return-of-premium programs, which return a portion or the entire premium upon the death of the LTC recipient.

The negative aspect of self-insuring is employing a care coordinator to help direct the family to find services.

Long-term Care for Veterans

If the individual is a US veteran, the Department of Veteran Affairs should be contacted. Based on the veteran's military service record and current situation, a veteran and his or her spouse may be eligible to receive compensation to pay for long-term care services at home or within the veteran hospital system.

There are only four types of people who can apply or help you apply for these benefits: the veteran, his or her legal representative, such as power of attorney, a VA authorized attorney, or the veteran benefit administrator (who can assist in the application process at no cost). It may be beneficial to have your estate and elder law attorney involved (many are VA accredited) in the process of applying. Oftentimes, reallocating assets in trusts can help you qualify. However, VA benefits can potentially impact Medicaid benefits in a negative way. You may be able to rearrange assets and qualify for VA benefits, but in the long run, it may be more beneficial to look at Medicaid benefits before jumping into something that could potentially hurt you and negatively impact your Medicaid eligibility.

A VA accredited attorney is helpful in weighing these options for you. Meeting with a person familiar with VA benefits and Medicaid should be explored in all circumstances.

Team Planning Your Retirement and Your Estate

Almost everyone would like to retire, enjoy life, and preserve his or her estate for the family. In today's world, creating and managing your retirement and estate plan often require a team of professionals. People work hard to accumulate their assets and need to make sure they are maximized. Building a team is essential for everyone that is planning to retire or has already retired.

Today's generation has more assets than ever before, and protecting them is imperative. Having a team of experts to guide you is essential. If you are building a home, then you work with a team of experts. You call an architect to design the home. The architect works in unison with the building contractor who coordinates with subcontractors. This makes perfect sense: a coordinated team of experts to help you achieve your goal. Building and preserving your financial assets work the same way. You need a coordinated team of financial and legal experts to help you achieve your financial goals.

Experts on Your Team

To help you navigate through this minefield, you need a lawyer, a tax advisor, an insurance agent, and in many cases, a person licensed in securities. Depending on your situation, you may need the entire team or just part of the team at any given time. Every situation is different. You may already have an attorney or CPA (Certified Public Accountant) that you are comfortable with and only need to add the two other professionals to complete your team. Or you may need to start from scratch.

Your attorney should specialize in estate planning and elder law. This means that he or she should be familiar not only with wills but also with different kinds of trust arrangements. In addition, your plan may include creating business entities, such as partnerships or limited liability companies, to protect your assets. You will need to make sure that your attorney is well versed in the planning techniques that include these types of entities.

You need to be prepared to discuss everything with your attorney—including your assets, your health conditions, past relationships, family members, disabilities, etc.

Your tax advisor should be at least a CPA who understands the tax and planning aspects of what your attorney may propose for your estate and should be able to offer additional suggestions as needed. In addition, the tax advisor must understand retirement funding vehicles, such as qualified retirement plans and annuities, as well as certain insurance products, such as life insurance and long-term care insurance. More important, the tax advisor should also be able to help you organize and coordinate your retirement funds so they are used to fund your living expenses in a tax-efficient manner.

The third member of your team, an insurance agent, structures and coordinates your insurance portfolio. The agent must understand the planning techniques proposed by your attorney and tax advisor and must have access to the appropriate insurance programs, such as life, disability, and long-term care insurances, as well as an understanding of Medicare, supplemental health, and prescription plans. He or she should have a strong knowledge of annuities with a vast number of annuities at his or her disposal.

The important thing to know about the insurance agent and investment advisor is that there are three types.

The first type of agent is a captured agent. A captured agent represents one company and can offer programs only from the company he or she represents. Captive agents may offer programs exclusive to their group.

The opposite of a captured agent is an independent agent who is able to represent any company and is often able to represent the same products as the captured agent (with the exception of exclusive programs). The independent agent is able to search and compare products.

The affiliated agent is not captive and not totally independent. He or she may or may not work under the umbrella of a captive agent or have the ability to offer other products and comparisons similar to an independent agent.

It is most important that your team work together to produce the best results for you. All members of the team must have one goal in mind: putting the best plan in place for you. They have to work together for you.

No matter what classification the industry puts on agents, the bottom line is the knowledge of the agent and his or her understanding of the dynamics of the plans and programs that will best fit your needs. For instance, 90 percent of all indexed annuities are the same. The remaining 10 percent are unique to your situation and are where your agent should command the program and be focused. Whole life policies follow the same general format with the exception of how you want the plan to perform based on the purpose of the plan.

The fourth member of your team is an investment advisor. An investment advisor can help to make sure your investment portfolio is properly structured, both inside and outside your retirement plan, which helps achieve your financial goals. It is important that the financial advisor has a complete understanding of when you want to have your investments placed into programs that are protected from market volatility and is willing to do so.

When to Assemble the Team, When to Start Accumulating for Retirement

It is always better to plan early; this will give you time to reevaluate your situation if things don't work out the way you expect. How many people have you spoken to that are unprepared to retire or wait until they are retiring to put a plan together? We see it often. Their method in this situation is to adjust their lifestyles to meet their income.

It is beneficial to establish retirement vehicles in your thirties or sooner to maximize and control your financial future. Retirement planning should begin with your first paycheck. Younger is always better. Modify your lifestyle to accumulate for retirement. After reading about qualified money, most people would probably look at accumulating non-qualified money in life insurance, annuities, or some type of a securities program instead of stuffing their qualified plan.

Some of these programs are based on age and health. The younger and healthier you are, the greater the accumulation. It is understood that things are going to happen, especially if or when you have a family, and at times, there may not be money to put away for retirement. Many of the suggestions made will help you through those difficult times by allowing you to access your funds. You can also stop and start contributing to these plans as you see fit. Remember you are in control. For people in their forties or fifties, there is still time to plan and prepare. A review of your accounts may prove wise. Structuring and turning qualified into non-qualified funds can help balance your portfolio. For people in their sixties who are planning to retire soon, finding the right professionals is imperative before starting retirement. The longer you wait and the closer you get to retirement, the fewer opportunities you have to maximize.

Putting together a team of professionals is essential to achieving your financial goals. If you have a team in place and each one understands his or her role and your goals, you will feel a great sense of relief knowing that you have maximized your financial potential and minimized your tax liability, all while protecting your assets and your family.

Please visit **www.Positioning4Retirement.com** and click on "Find a Professional" to begin organizing your team.

RESOURCES

The following resources have been used in this book. In addition, you will find many of them useful for further information and edification. The IRS publications, in particular, are valuable references; they are reviewed periodically and kept up to date.

Anspach, Dana. "Social Security for Widows and Widowers." About.com. http://moneyover55.about.com/od/SocialSecuritySurvivorBenefits/a/Social-Security-For-Widows-And-Widowers.htm.

———. "Large Cap Stock Market Return Since 1973." About.com. moneyover55.com/od/howtoinvest/a/marketreturns.htm.

Banerjee, Sudipto. "Effects of Nursing Home Stays on Household Portfolios." EBRI Issue Brief, no. 372, June 2012.

"Facts from EBRI—History of 401(k) Plans: An Update." Databook on Employee Benefits, 4th Edition. Washington, DC: Employee Benefit Research Institute, 1997.

IRS Publications
    560 Retirement Plans for Small Businesses (SEP, SIMPLE, and Qualified
        Plans)
    571 Tax-Sheltered Annuity Plans (403(b) Plans) for Employees of Public
        Schools and Certain Tax-Exempt Organizations
    575 Pension and Annuity Income
    590 Individual Retirement Arrangements (IRAs); includes in Appendix
        C the Life Expectancy Tables
    939 General Rule for Pensions and Annuities
    Bulletin 2013-47
    Contributing to a Designated Roth Account
    Designated Roth Accounts
    IRS Code 72(t)(q)
    Roth Comparison Chart

Top Ten Differences between a Roth IRA and a Designated Roth Account, Template 1102CL (11-2012)

Kitces, Michael. "Dodging the Income Limit on Roth Contributions—Strategy or Abuse?" Kitces.com, January 24, 2012.

Lassiter, Mark. "Social Security Publishes New Rule Revising Withdrawal Policy" News Release. SSA Press Office. December 8, 2010.

National Association of Insurance Commissioners (NAIC) publications
    Buyer's Guide to Fixed Deferred Annuities with Appendix for Equity-Indexed Annuities, 2007
    Life Insurance Buyer's Guide, 2007
    A Shopper's Guide to Long-Term Care Insurance (updated annually)

"Qualified Terminable Interest Property Trust (QTIP)." The Wealth Counselor LLC.

Slott, Ed. "Ask Ed Slott: Explaining the Step Transaction Doctrine." Financial Planning.com, April 27, 2011.

Social Security Administration publications
    Government Pension Offset, No. 05-10007
    How Social Security Can Help You When A Family Member Dies, No. 05-10008
    How State And Local Government Employees Are Covered By Social Security And Medicare, No. 05-10051
    Military Service And Social Security, No. 05-10017
    News Release, Social Security Publishes New Rule Revising Withdrawal Policy Also Limit Voluntary Suspensions to Prospective Months, No. SSA-2009-0073
    Retirement Benefits, No. 05-10035
    Special Payments After Retirement, No. 05-10063
    When to Start Receiving Retirement Benefits, No. 05-10146
    Windfall Elimination Provision, No. 05-10045

Steiner, Bruce D. "Trusts as Beneficiaries of Retirement Benefits." Tax Management Estates, Gifts And Trust Journal, vol. 29, no. 2, March 11, 2004.

"Step Transaction Doctrine." Wikipedia. http://en.wikipedia.org/wiki/Step_transaction_doctrine.

Taylor, Philip. "The Backdoor to Making a Roth IRA Contribution." PT Money, October 9, 2012.

"Toward a More Complete 401(k) History." EBRI Notes, vol. 24, no. 12, December 2003.

United States Department of Labor, Employee Benefits Security Administration. "401(k) Plans for Small Businesses." www.dol.gov/ebsa/pdf/irspub4222.pdf.

"Using an Annuity to Keep the Spouse of a Medicaid Applicant from Becoming Impoverished." ElderLawAnswers (modified 12/13/2013), http://www.elderlawanswers.com/using-an-annuity-to-keep-the-spouse-of-a-medicaid-applicant-from-becoming-impoverished-12480.

U.S. Securities and Exchange Commission. "Variable Annuities: What You Should Know." www.sec.gov/investor/pubs/varannty.htm.

"What is a Modified Endowment Contract (MEC)?" Advice Center/Family Life (reprinted from Forefield, Inc.), August 8, 2008.